D1038003

The Right Distance

The Right Distance

Distance

SAMUEL F. PICKERING, JR.

THE UNIVERSITY OF GEORGIA PRESS
ATHENS AND LONDON

© 1987 by the University of Georgia Press
Athens, Georgia 30602
All rights reserved
Designed by Joanna V. Hill
Set in Linotron Primer
The paper in this book meets the guidelines for
permanence and durability of the Committee on
Production Guidelines for Book Longevity of the Council
on Library Resources.

Printed in the United States of America
91 90 89 88 87   5 4 3 2 1

LIBRARY OF CONGRESS CATALOGING IN
PUBLICATION DATA

Pickering, Samuel F., 1941–
    The right distance.
    I. Title.
AC8.P67   1987   081   86–16012
ISBN 0–8203–0906–0 (alk. paper)

BRITISH LIBRARY CATALOGING IN
PUBLICATION DATA AVAILABLE

For my children
Francis, Edward, and Eliza

Contents

Acknowledgments

The author and the publisher gratefully acknowledge the following publications, in which essays in this volume first appeared:

Chariton Review: "Getting It"
Chicago Review: "The Right Distance"
Negative Capability: "Advice and Dissent"
North Dakota Quarterly: "Loose Ends"
Southern Review: "Pictures"
Southwest Review: "Too Late"
Texas Review: "Country Life," "Particulars," "Being Familiar"
Virginia Quarterly Review: "Just Started," "Son and Father,"
   "Ink Blots"

The Right Distance

Being Familiar

Last spring I published a familiar essay in the *Kenyon Review*. The essay contained some untoward parts, and for a while I thought about suppressing it. Eventually, though, I decided that no one in my family was liable to read the *Kenyon Review*. I was mistaken. Like sin, words will out, particularly if they involve, as mine did, youthful indiscretions. A week after the essay appeared, Mother telephoned. A friend, she informed me, sent her the *Review*. The essay had not gone down well in Tennessee. "We are," Mother said, "people of some reputation in this town, and this kind of thing."

Before she could sink her teeth into the piece and shake it back and forth, I interrupted. "Mamma," I said, straining to change the grounds of conversation, "Mamma, don't think of the essay as truth; think of it as literature."

"Literature," Mother exclaimed after a slight pause, "it's not literature. It's bullshit!"

Mother's reaction was not surprising. In my essays being familiar means being personal and approachable. My life furnishes matter for writing, and although my essays don't always describe

I

what really happened, they often strike readers as true. Unlike members of my family, who, understandably enough, are often embarrassed by my writing, readers are generally attracted. Being personal makes me approachable, and they write me almost as a friend, in the process brightening my days and giving me material for more essays. "Mr. Pickering," a woman wrote this September, "You don't know us, but we are a black preacher and wife from Tennessee—Waverley, Tennessee. So I thought if you had the time you might want to come to our Fiftieth Wedding Anniversary. We would be glad to see someone from Tennessee." Accompanying the letter was a gold-and-claret invitation from the couple's children and grandchildren and the members of the minister's congregation, inviting me to the "joyful Fiftieth Wedding Celebration." Although the day of the celebration was cold and rainy, the mood inside the church was warm and sunny. Carrying a ring, a little boy dressed in white nervously picked his way down the aisle. Behind him skipped a small girl, plucking petals from daisies, all the while saying "He loves me" and "She loves me."

Although I often spend days wandering about in old graveyards, picnicking and reading tombstones, I had not been in a church for a long time. I no longer believe, and although I long for faith, I avoid churches. I am afraid of entering that world redolent with sweet memories—birthday parties for the baby Jesus, mite boxes, and soothing calls to Abide with Him. Once within the fold I might not have will enough to kick loose. Instead of living the sad joy of this dark earth, I might spend my time dreaming of life to come. The pull of church, though, is strong, and at the end of the celebration when a big woman stood up and sang the Lord's Prayer, I almost cried. For a moment, years and hard-edged knowledge fell away. I saw myself in Sunday school, an awkward little boy in a gray coat and gray short pants, wonderfully happy as he looked at a silver star beside his name on an attendance chart.

I don't attend all the celebrations to which I am invited, but I try to go to most. Sometimes being approachable leads to physical rather than mental pain. Occasionally I run road races. I don't run for prizes. I am remarkably slow afoot; what is a sprint to me is a crawl to the young and the fleet. In truth, if I were fast, I would probably stop running. Competition makes me uncomfortable, and I labor to avoid it. Road races are simply my excuse for traveling around New England, breathing the salt air along the Maine coast and wandering through the green-and-white villages of Vermont. In my essays on running, losers appear wise; at the back of the pack, I argue, a person has time to look around, to talk, and to appreciate. Probably because they, too, have not won a race, many people like the essays. As a result a race director will sometimes ask me to run in his race. In October I was invited to a half-marathon in New Hampshire. "A road race entry from the Lone Ranger of Running," the director wrote, "would boost morale and increase the respectability of the race, especially if you happen to be old." The letter was light and seductive. "Your personal safety," the director continued, "will be guaranteed. Several hours before the race, police will arrest all those citizens with a previous history of gunplay involving joggers, and the Dog Officer will cudgel all loose dogs on the route itself."

Although I had not run thirteen miles in eight years, I began training. "There is no telling what this will lead to," I told my wife, Vicki, when she said I was too old and fat for such a race; "maybe a running magazine will make me a correspondent."

"The only thing this is going to lead to," she answered, "is the bed." Alas, she was right. One afternoon a week before the race as I ran up a tall hill, my heel began to ache. The next morning my Achilles tendon was as hard and as thick as a two-by-four. Six weeks have passed, and the Lone Ranger of Running still has trouble mounting the stairs in his house, much less hills in New England.

Beginning an essay is difficult. Unlike academic writing, for which one can imagine a specific audience and which generates its own urgency, pushing a person to put his thoughts down before someone else gets the same idea, the writer of familiar essays feels little compulsion to write. Often about the inconsequential, the familiar essay adds nothing to knowledge. No experts wait, minds sharpened, ready to cut and slice and then weigh the learning and find it wanting. Unable to imagine particular readers and under no pressure to publish, the essayist is tempted to live ordinary life rather than to write about it. I planned to spend last Saturday writing, but when Vicki said she wanted to visit local church bazaars to search for Christmas presents and asked me to mind the children, I gladly put my pencils aside and turned to other things. Two years ago I bought three cords of firewood. Although the woodsman assured me that it was split, much of the wood consisted of logs fit more for factory heating plants than living-room stoves. This year I purchased a maul, and while the children spun up and down the driveway on Big Wheels, I split wood.

Splitting wood is remarkably satisfying. There is something heartily primitive about wresting logs out from the bottom of an old woodpile and then smashing them into splinters. I like my maul, but while splitting wood I dreamed about a chainsaw. Most of my friends own them, but Vicki won't let me have one. Whenever my friends use their saws, they wear caps—tough caps that belie their ages and sit boldly on their heads, proclaiming in black letters Echo or Stihl. I would like such a cap. By comparison my only hat seems weak and intellectual. It is a tweedy, checkered English cap. On top is a big brown spot. One day after the cap got soaked in a storm, I hung it on a lamp to dry. Unfortunately, heat from the light bulb burned it, not badly enough for me to throw it away but badly enough to leave a mark everybody notices.

By the time Vicki came home, I had split most of the wood, at least all I was going to split. I did not, however, settle down to writing. That morning Tom, the UPS man, delivered a box of peonies from Spring Hill Nurseries in Tipp City, Ohio. Since the weather was good and rain was forecast for Sunday, after lunch I dug holes for the peonies along the edge of the driveway. Then when Vicki went to Ledgecrest to buy bone meal, the children and I went into the woods behind the house, and I dug up several cartloads of rich, black humus for the holes. Digging, carting, and planting took most of the afternoon, and I put off writing until after dinner. I didn't expect to get much done; something always comes up after dinner, and, sure enough, while I was looking through my notebooks, Vicki called from the kitchen. Edward, our two-and-a-half-year-old, had stuck a raisin up his nose. Instead of blowing as Vicki instructed, Edward snorted, and snorted like a bull let out to cows in the spring. And the raisin which had once hung loosely in mid-passage took off and, flying upward like a rocket, was now firmly lodged beyond the reach of tweezers, ready and indeed eager, I was sure, to dive into Edward's sinuses. I did not know what to do, but since Edward was screaming, Vicki said we had to try something. I carried Edward into the living room and stretched him out on a sofa. Vicki got a toothpick and then went harpooning. I held Edward down with one hand; with the other I pried open his nose. In my mouth was a flashlight; by humping over I was able to shine it in the general vicinity of Edward's face. Although Vicki proved herself a master harpooner and quickly speared the raisin, the excitement wore me out, making me fit only for television.

Since Sunday was supposed to be rainy, I had every intention of writing. Unpredictably, though, Sunday dawned warm and bright and was much too pretty to spend at a desk. After breakfast Vicki, the boys, and Eliza and I set out on a walk. Since she was only six months old, Eliza rode in a baby carrier strapped to my back. We crossed Horsebarn Hill on the university farm and, cutting through fields of newly harvested corn, drifted toward the Fenton River. *Drifted* is the right word. Direction, like my determination to write, came and went. The boys explored the fields and found several half-eaten ears of hard, yellow corn. For the boys the corn was golden treasure, and soon I looked like a scarecrow with shucks sticking out of my pockets. In the trees along one side of the field grew bittersweet; we noted it and said we would return later and pick some. At the edge of another field grew pokeberries. I crushed a handful, and after telling the boys that Cherokee Indians used them to make ink, I painted my face. Much to Vicki's dismay, the boys did the same. Earlier in the fall, a hurricane tore through Connecticut, and throughout the woods lay the broken tops of oak trees, bushy with dried leaves and heavy with acorns. These, too, were judged treasure, and I crammed handfuls into my pockets along with the corn.

The woods were quiet, and except for the sounds of our walking, we heard little. I have never seen or heard an owl in the wild, and I hoped I might see one sitting wide-eyed, deep in the hollow of a rotten tree. I didn't, and nothing appeared to mark place or time until Edward suddenly plopped heavily down on the ground. He was worn out. To get him going again, I promised to buy him a treat at the university's ice cream bar. For a while he stumbled along, but then he collapsed for good. I picked him up and, turning back through the woods, took what I hoped was a short cut home. My sense of direction is pretty good, and soon we were back at the cornfields. Near the edge of the fields grew cattails, ready to go to seed. Ducking down, I crawled through a hole in the fence and picked one. When I rubbed it, the seeds with their long silky tails burst out and, catching the breeze, blew around us like snow. Next I saw some cockleburs; I picked a handful and, sticking them on Francis's shirt, made a smiling face. Just then, Vicki looked at Eliza; blood ran down Eliza's forehead. A wire had scraped the top of her head when I crawled under the fence. All plans for the dairy bar were off, and we hurried home. Before we got there, Francis began to scream. Prickles on the cockleburs worked through his sweater and shirt and irritated his chest, making his skin break out in red bumps. As soon as we were home, I bathed Francis with calamine lotion, and Vicki cleaned Eliza's cut with hydrogen peroxide. This bothered me because I thought Vicki ought to use an ointment crammed with antibiotics. "You will have only yourself to blame if she gets lockjaw and dies," I said and went to read Dr. Spock on tetanus. And so the day passed. Again I did not write, although I eventually went to the dairy bar. The boys and I ate fudge-cake sundaes, hot fudge poured over chocolate ice cream and a piece of fudge. For her part Vicki had an apple sundae, apple ice cream buried under a thick applesauce topping. The weekend's having gone by with my writing nothing did not bother me. Rarely does the familiar essay set out hiking boots afoot and compass in hand; instead it meanders, picking cockleburs and cattails, hoping to see an owl and eating ice cream. Over the years I have grown accustomed to its ways and satisfied with an easy, meandering life. I don't know whether the essay has influenced me, or whether writing it has just coincided with the growth of family and the slowing of my own pace. Whatever the case, faraway places with their sounding cataracts and stony castles no longer attract me. Living at home is good enough. In the fall I look forward to Vicki's tying an orange ribbon around Indian corn and hanging the corn on the front door. On the stoop she puts pots of yellow chrysanthemums; in late spring she puts out red and, if she can get them, white geraniums; in summer, first pansies, then marigolds. In ordinary life I now find the stuff of poetry and research. Almost everything, even a day's dull walk, can be matter for a familiar essay.

This fall when the weather turned cold, scores of insects rushed to my house for shelter. Since they were little, Vicki and I generally ignored them. The only time we were really aware of them was at night. The ceiling of our bedroom seemed to be a gathering place. Before turning out the light, Vicki and I stretched out and watched them rush busily about. Occasionally one tumbled off the ceiling and landed scurrying on the covers. Often the insects that fell were click beetles or, as they have also been known, spring bugs, blacksmiths, and skipjacks. For years I caught them in the house and tossed them outside without a thought. Now under the influence of the familiar essay I looked at them closely and wondered how such small creatures could jump so fast and so high. One morning shortly afterwards I went to the bug section of the university library. I soon realized how little I knew about my everyday world. Among the ordinary inhabitants of my bedroom, the little click beetle was extraordinary. Compared to him the world's best high jumper is a stumbling amateur. When the beetle jumps, his speed is eight feet per second; not only that but while in the air he does up to six end-over-end somersaults. To get off the ground, he snaps the top half of his body forward. The motion resembles that of the old-fashioned wooden mousetrap. When a mouse takes the cheese and releases the catch, the trap's arm flies up and over, pulling the trap into the air. In less than two thousandths of a second, the upper half of the beetle's body moves in a similar fashion, accelerating to several hundred times the force of gravity, pulling him off the ground. When he is dozing or just visiting with acquaintances, a small peg on the upper part of the beetle keeps his body straight. A catch holds the peg in place until the beetle decides to jump. When the catch is released, the peg slams forward into a pocket on the lower part of the beetle's body. It slams into the pocket so hard that it makes a snapping sound.

There are over five hundred varieties of click beetles in the United States. The small suburban family with its two children, a marble cat, and a dachshund is not for the click beetle. Since it spends three to five years underground, feeding on roots and tubers, few people, aside from farmers and gardeners, know just how prolific the beetle is. Called wire worms, the young of some varieties flourish in wild numbers. If the wire worms on an acre of land are fewer than three hundred thousand, an agricultural journal stated, almost any crop can be planted. Cereals, but not potatoes, can be grown on land that contains more than three but less than six hundred thousand wire worms per acre. When the worms number more than six hundred thousand, it is difficult to grow any crop on light soil. On heavy soil, barley is likely to succeed. Beyond a million worms per acre, no matter what the texture of the soil, no crop can be grown.

The information that I found in the library fascinated me, and that night as Vicki and I lay in bed, watching our visitors traipse about, I told her what I had learned. For a time she was interested, or at least she pretended to be interested, until I started talking about the number of wire worms on an acre of land. "That's enough about beetles," she said, turning off the light; "three children is enough for man or bug. That's all we have, and that's all we are going to have. You had better study something less prolific. Good night."

Although familiar essays have changed the way I live, even creeping into the bedroom on six legs, they have not increased the size of my family. Some things are beyond the power of the pen. What the essays have influenced, though, is my academic career. Scholarly writing and the familiar essay are very different. Instead of driving hard to prove a point, the essay saunters, letting the writer follow the vagaries of his own willful curiosity. Instead of reaching conclusions, the essay ruminates and wonders. Rather than being right or informative, it is thoughtful. Instead of being serious, it is often lighthearted, pondering subjects like the breeding habits of beetles, and, alas, of people. Of course as a person ages it becomes increasingly difficult to be scholarly or definitive. Truth seems beside the point, or at least amid the many doings of a day it seems to have progressively less to do with living. Years have passed since I have read a study advertised as definitive. Being definitive, and perhaps even clever, is an activity for youth. Certainly it was in my case. Not long ago a university press that just reprinted an academic book I wrote in fresher days rejected a new manuscript. "You don't reach enough conclusions," the editor explained; "writing essays seems to have affected your scholarship." The editor was right; I now have trouble reaching conclusions. Instead of cudgeling stray dogs along the route I travel, as the director of that half-marathon in New Hampshire promised, I stop and pet them. If they could talk, I'd probably sit down, start chatting, and forget about the race.

Miss Dotty Brice lived in the small town in which my father grew up. The daughter of Shubael Brice, who owned the hardware store, Miss Dotty never married. An only child, she lived at home and nursed her parents to the grave. Shubael Brice was not a good businessman, and at his death when the store was sold and the debts paid off, Miss Dotty was left with little. Over the years her little shrank to nothing; yet she never went without. Relatives mended her roof, and neighbors brought her firewood and coal, chickens and eggs. Several nights a week at dinnertime, Miss Dotty put on her best clothes and started uptown. The townspeople watched for her, and before she walked far, someone always invited her in for dinner. "Don't you look nice, Miss Dotty," a neighbor would say; "we are just sitting down to eat. We are not having anything fancy, but we'd be pleased if you would join us." Like Miss Dotty, the familiar essay isn't a rich literary form. It doesn't have much of its own, yet it never goes wanting. Whenever writing time rolls around, it starts ambling along and before it has gotten far from the front stoop it has met someone or something and is sitting down at the table, head bowed, ready for life's blessings.

The Right Distance

When I was small, my maternal grandfather owned a dairy farm in Hanover, Virginia, a little town north of Richmond. Early one morning during the Second World War, not long after the Germans attacked Egypt, Henry Hackenbridge, our herdsman, knocked on the kitchen door and asked to speak to Grandfather. "Mr. Ratcliffe," he said, "the Germans are getting mighty close. I heard they bombed Alexandria last night. Shouldn't we move the cows?" Twenty years have passed since I was a camp counselor in Maine. Unlike the Potomac, Sebago Lake can't be confused with the Nile, yet like Henry, I have trouble getting the right distance on things. The smell of damp pine woods and the sound of loons calling in the morning cling to me, and occasionally, after I have gone to bed early and slept well, I bound up at dawn eager for a skinny dip.

My closest friend in Maine was Alan Chadwick, an athlete bright with ability and intelligence. After my last summer at camp, I went to Britain and Alan to California. Our paths did not cross again until this spring, when I stopped for a traffic light in Mystic, Connecticut. The light was long and I passed the time looking at people on the sidewalk. Suddenly I saw Alan. His hair was gray; he had put on thirty pounds; but I would have known him anywhere. I blew my horn and pulled over to the side of the road. Alan recognized me and came over. We decided to have a drink in the Mystic Tavern and as we walked there memories of hellion summers ran through my mind. Long before streaking became popular, Alan was an expert at Stark Walks and Nudeathons. At Prout's Neck and Reid State Park, we strolled arm in arm along the beach, stopping to chat with swimmers, asking if they had seen two bathing suits. Sharks, we said, had bitten ours off. Later, after avoiding wardens and policemen, we nursed sunburns, drank Casco Bay ginger ale, and ate fried clams and dollar-and-a-quarter lobsters. Night after night we double-dated, going to spots we called the Peanut Butter Grove, Crescent Lake Beach, and the Sawdust Pits. There we told stories, laughed, and, if we were lucky, got an innocent kiss or two. Other nights we bought Colt 45 and walked down the old logging road. Stretched out in the sand, we drank and talked about all those things we thought men talked about: the women we said we had had and of course hadn't and the people we said we would become and didn't. We swore that when we met in the future we would fight until one of us admitted the other was the better man. Afterwards, we would roll time back on a wheel of wonderful stories.

"Alan," I said as we sat down in a booth in the tavern, "what have you been doing for twenty years? Apart," I added, "from serious eating."

"This isn't food, Sam," he answered patting his stomach, "this is booze, and aside from two wives and four DWIs, I haven't done much."

My father is from Carthage, Tennessee, a small town high on a bluff above the Cumberland River. In Carthage, Earl Hodges owned a couple of acres of land, a few peach trees, a mule and a plough, and a still. The land was played out, the peach trees spindly and the mule old and not fit for ploughing. But the still was good, and Earl made a living selling whiskey. Periodically the sheriff arrested him and he had to appear before Judge Joe Russell. Earl was a master at getting off; once he fainted in the courtroom and the county clerk had to take him to the doctor. Although the family was distinguished and almost single-handedly supported the Methodist church in town, Judge Russell had a disreputable brother, Jerry, who patronized Earl and his still. On one occasion the sheriff arrested Earl while Jerry was asleep in Earl's cabin. "You've been selling whiskey again," Judge Joe said later in the courtroom.

"No sir," Earl answered.

Looking intently at him, Judge Russell asked, "On such and such a day, didn't Mr. Jerry Russell come to your place and buy half a gallon of whiskey and stay dead drunk for two days?"

Earl started to fidget and then said nervously, "Which Mr.— which Mr. Russell was that?" People in the courtroom began to laugh; the case was adjourned, and Earl eventually got off.

Like Earl, I hoped vagueness would save the day, and I turned the conversation away from drink to old friends. Alan would not know much about them, I thought, and we could spend the day comfortably in the cool shade of memory. "What in the world," I asked, "has happened to Cary, Steve, and Townsend?"

"Poor Cary," Alan began and then told a sad tale of sickness and divorce. Townsend, he told me, had drowned off Martha's Vineyard while fishing. Happily, Alan knew only that Steve was teaching in Boston. As we sat talking, light seemed to drain away and mortality weighed heavy. We tried to recall the times we spent together, but our enthusiasm was false, and things fell apart. Eventually Alan told me about his wives, the jobs he left, and his problem with drink. I told him about the academic chairs that folded beneath me, and we missed connections. As we got up to go, I wanted to grab Alan, hug him, and say, "Boy, man, or memory, I'll always love you and the things we shared." Of course I didn't; I didn't know how. Instead we shook hands and agreed that it had been a long time since we had seen each other. "Too long," we chorused; "let's not let it happen again." We promised to get together.

"Call me the next time you are near," I said, giving him my telephone number in Storrs.

"Damn straight," Alan answered and gave me his address in Vermont.

I haven't seen Alan since. Strangely, though, my thoughts gathered momentum and ran along happily after the meeting. As I remembered the things Alan and I once did together, the past became the present, and life glowed warmly. Like hope, affection springs eternal, and although years had pushed their way between Alan and me, I decided to find Steve in Boston. For two summers we had been inseparable. One June I bought rubber idiot masks in a fun shop in Portland. At night we fastened the masks to the backs of our heads, put our shirts on backwards, and drove along the highway. We sat sideways in the front seat, and as soon as a car approached from behind, we started bouncing up and down. Usually the driver turned on his high beams and saw two idiots staring at him. Often the driver pulled off the road or turned around and drove rapidly back where he came from.

Once, at noon, Steve and I donned shorts and striped T-shirts and, carrying all-day lollipops, set out for Longfellow's statue in Portland. When we got there, we climbed onto his knees and began to lick the lollipops and recite poetry. A crowd gathered and we stayed for three-quarters of an hour. Then a man, worse for drink, stumbled off the curb and began hectoring us. A siren wailed in the distance, and we left. Twenty years ago Portland was an easygoing town ripe for fun. One day Steve and I led a crew of counselors to the army surplus store. There we bought old uniforms and put them on. Next we purchased a huge shell casing, or so it seemed. Four of us picked it up, and off we went. Two "soldiers" cleared the sidewalks ahead and behind, warning pedestrians to beware the "unexploded shell." For almost an hour we wandered through Portland, stopping traffic and clearing sidewalks. In those days no beast lurked within; it was external, a mask or costume to be worn for fun, not an internal state of mind. I found Steve's name in the Boston telephone directory. As I dialed his number, I wondered what had happened to the old wild man. When Steve himself answered the telephone, I greeted him with a long string of over-ripe words. "Who, who is this?" he said tentatively.

"Why, you scalawag," I answered, "don't you remember your buddy Sam?"

There was a long pause; then a voice I didn't recognize asked, "Sam, are you a Christian?"

For me Maine is not now so much a place as it is a state of existence, sentimentalized as a time of pure delight. The actual place I knew has changed. Panther Pond has become Panther Lake, and lobster pounds have become boutiques. If identity is bound firmly to place, then one will suffer because places disappear. My father grew up in a Victorian house near the center of Carthage. Huge sugar maples filled the front yard. In the back were sheds and a barn and long lazy fields stretching down to the Cumberland River. Life was slow in Carthage, and early in the morning Grandfather walked uptown and drank coffee with his friends. Breakfast waited until he returned. My father left Carthage for good after college. Not long ago, though, Father and I went back for a funeral. For Father the funeral was for more than a friend; the town he knew was also dead. Grandfather's sugar maples had been cut down in order to widen the main street. A brick duplex had been built in the vacant lot on the right of Father's home, while a funeral home had replaced the old house on the other side. The sheds and barn had disappeared, and the back field had become a trailer park.

Memories resemble anchors embedded deep in the ocean floor, and, unlike places, they resist the turbulence of years. From them chain continuity and comfort. I teach in a university and occasionally write essays. Instead of examining a single topic, my essays meander, pausing whenever anything attracts me. Stories always crop up in my writings, and pruning can't keep them from sprouting between rows of thought. Behind the stories lie my summers in Maine. I told my first tales as a camp counselor. I sat on a low stool in the middle of my cabin and wore a flying cap which I had bought in the army surplus store. In it I wrote "Wilbur Ratcliffe" and told the campers that it belonged to my great-uncle. He had worn it during the First World War. He was an ace, I said, and had shot down the Red Baron but had been too modest to correct history.

While I sat on the stool, the campers waved their flashlights about like searchlights scanning the sky for zeppelins. Eventually the flying cap became a thinker's cap, and I came down to earth to begin trips to far-off lands. Some nights I went to the ends of the universe; other nights I stayed home and galloped across the prairie ahead of bands of bloodthirsty desperadoes. My favorite hero was Enoch Catlin, known to his friends as "Nuk." Adventure followed Nuk like his shadow. Once Barbary pirates captured him. He was imprisoned and endured unspeakable tortures without flinching until one day he wrung the neck of a guard and escaped. A horde of villains pursued him through the winding bazaar, waving scimitars and shouting fiendishly. Finding no place to hide, Nuk sprinted through the courtyard of a mosque and darted up the stairs of the minaret. At the top he tore a dagger from the hand of a mullah and threw him down the steps, bowling over his pursuers. Then standing on the edge of the minaret, he sprang to the city wall and dropped to the ground on the other side. Before him stretched the desert, its sands broken only by the silhouette of an occasional date palm. Capture was inevitable unless Nuk found a place to hide. Demon drink had my friend Alan in its clutches. Realistically, escape seemed impossible, and after our conversation I could not imagine a happy ending to his life. In my stories of twenty years ago nothing was impossible. My heroes always threw off the monsters which pursued them and became stronger. Just beyond the wall loomed a mountain of bones, grim testimonial to the pirates' bar-

barity. Without a pause, Nuk jumped into the pile and buried his body almost completely, leaving only his nose and mouth exposed in order to breathe.

When the pirates ran through the main gate of the city, they saw no sign of Nuk. His disappearance frightened them, and, concluding that he was a genie, they hurried back to the city and locked the gates behind them. Nuk seized the chance and set off across the desert. He did not escape unmarked, however. While he lay amid the carrion, a vulture lit on the pile, bit his nose off, and swallowed it. The pirates would have noticed movement, and drawing upon inner reserves of true grit, Nuk remained still. After his pursuers turned back, Nuk grabbed the vulture, wrung its neck, and, cramming his hand down its gullet, extracted his nose, not too much the worse for digestion. Nuk then had many incredible adventures in a mask. Eventually, after a wizard rubbed it with "adder grease" and mumbled an enchantment, Nuk's nose was reattached to his face, and like all the just and the brave he retired to live happily ever after.

Henry Hackenbridge occasionally drank. Once when he went too far, Grandfather called the sheriff. A night in the Hanover jail, Grandfather thought, would do him good. The next morning while we were eating breakfast, Henry telephoned. "Mr. Ratcliffe," he said, "come and get me out of this jail. The coffee is no good and the cream is sour." The interior of the Mystic Tavern was dark. As Alan talked it was difficult to get the right distance on things. The present seemed a prison, and our words curdled. When we said goodbye and left, I was relieved. This summer, though, for the first time in twenty years, I am going to visit Maine. I tell friends I am going because my little boy Francis will soon be old enough for camp. "Summers," I say, "are important for a youngster. I want to look at several camps and pick out the best for Francis." I won't look hard, of course, and I'll visit only one camp, Camp Timanous in Raymond, Maine. And I am not going for my son; I'm going for myself. Maybe some of my old friends will be there looking for camps for their sons. Grant might turn up. I know he must have done well. He and I once took twelve eight-year-olds on a canoe trip. We forgot the butter and the syrup for the pancakes. That worked out fine, though. We mixed Kool-Aid with the batter and made batches of red, purple, and green pancakes and called them spacecakes. The kids loved them. We also forgot the tents and it rained. What we did was amazing, a stroke of genius. I took . . .

Particulars

Nobody in Carthage, Tennessee, believed Cousin James Ligon would marry. One hot summer, though, when he was forty, James moved to Nashville. By September he had a wife. James did not introduce her around Carthage, and naturally people wondered what she was like. Not long after the marriage my grandfather met old Mr. Ligon on the street. After discussing the weather, tobacco, and local Republican doings, grandfather brought up the marriage.

"Knowing James as I do," he said, "I'm satisfied he married a fine person."

"Yes, indeed, Sam," Mr. Ligon replied. "Of course there are a couple of particulars. She's older than James. She's been married before. She's a nurse, and she's a Catholic."

Often particulars are not simply greater than wholes but remarkably different, and the person who strides along contemplating grand designs is certain to tumble over small details. Twenty years ago in graduate school—before grass seed and lawn mowers, strollers and car seats—my friends and I spent much energy plotting the bedding of women. We began countless conspiracies and had marvelous times; the only thing that eluded us was success.

One afternoon a physicist friend burst into my room, waving a piece of paper. "I've got it now," he shouted, "the Eighteen Steps to Seduction, drawn up according to scientific method and guaranteed not to fail."

"What are the steps?" I asked.

"Never you mind," he said; "tonight I am testing it out."

The next morning at breakfast, he looked a little glum. "How did you do?" I asked.

"Tripped on Step Two," he said, adding hurriedly, "Nothing is wrong with the plan that a little tinkering won't set right." I don't know whether my friend ever perfected his plan. He has been married now for a long time, but since his wife, like that of Cousin James, is a good bit older, I suspect that if the romance involved a plan, it was hers, not his.

In life a person has got to keep a weather eye cocked for particulars. Unfortunately, as one grows older, he becomes careless. Recently the English department in which I teach interviewed people for a job. The head of the search committee sent a note around asking for volunteers to eat meals with the candidates. Thinking I ought to do something but not wanting to spend much time doing it, I gave no thought to particulars and volunteered for breakfast. Eggs and bacon, even when stretched out by two cups of coffee, I calculated, disappeared quickly and did not lend themselves to protracted conversation. Shortly after I volunteered, the head of the search committee sent me a note. "Dear Sam," he wrote, "Could you deliver Jones to Bradley Field Wed. morning for his flight at 7:30 A.M.? You could have breakfast with him and probe for weaknesses—or something." The only way I could have eaten breakfast with Jones was to have flown to Wisconsin with him. Tuesday night there was a snowstorm, and I left home at 4:30 in order to get to the airport on time. The roads were so slippery that I did more praying than probing.

"To heck with his weaknesses," my wife, Vicki, said when I

returned, reporting I had discovered little about Jones. "You have driven candidates across the state, but have you," she asked, "ever been invited to eat a real meal with one?"

"No," I started, "but . . ."

"There are no *buts* to this," she broke in; "you have a distinguished record, or so you say, and you are paid peanuts and treated like a chauffeur. Whenever there is something inconvenient to be done, people call on you. 'Good old soft Sam'—why don't you say no? Just for once, be nasty. It will do you a world of good."

Although I did not tell her, Vicki was wrong. A dozen years ago I had been nasty about something academic, and although success brought pleasure, a little bit of which remains even today, it also left guilt behind. When I began teaching, I thought that most people approved my work. Eventually, however, I discovered that not only was I mistaken but one person felt so strongly that he wrote a number of harsh letters about me, all the while professing admiration to my face. This irritated me, and I decided that if an opportunity arose, I would pay him back. Not long afterward I changed jobs; soon after that I was invited to speak at a western university. At a dinner party the evening after my talk, the chairman of the English department told me that recently he had received a job application from one of my former colleagues. It was the very man who had written the uncomplimentary letters. "Both he and his wife," the chairman said, "have applied for posts. On paper they look first-rate and at the moment are our leading candidates. What," he added, "are they really like?"

"Oh, paper doesn't lie," I answered; "they are both splendid and would make superb colleagues and be distinguished additions to your department." After making certain that my praise had attracted the attention of everyone about the table, I went on, "There is one particular about her, but I hesitate to mention it."

"What is it?" the chairman asked. "We, of course, will treat anything you say as confidential."

"Well," I began, "you have been so extraordinarily gracious to me that I would feel bad if I were not entirely honest with you. She is," I said, lowering my voice, "a little contentious and if thwarted in any way is liable to accuse the department of sexism and sue the university."

I have written much about literature. When I began to write, I was careful and painstakingly raised interpretations upon a sturdy foundation of facts. Nowadays I am not particular about my particulars. In an important scene in Charlotte Brontë's novel *Jane Eyre,* Jane wandered alone on a romantic midsummer evening into the garden at Thornfield, the estate of her employer, Rochester. While she was in the garden, Rochester appeared mysteriously and, despite being married, courted her. Last year in a Baptist church I heard the hymn "In the Garden." "I come to the garden alone, / While the dew is still on the roses," Charles Miles, the author, wrote,

> And the voice I hear falling on my ear,
> The Son of God discloses.
> And He walks with me, and He talks with me,
> And He tells me I am His own;
> And the joy we share as we tarry there,
> None other has ever known.

The events of "In the Garden" closely parallel those that occurred when Jane met Rochester in the garden at Thornfield. Since Charlotte Brontë's father was a minister, since she had read evangelical publications like the *Methodist Magazine* when she was young, and since Christian themes and symbols were central in her novels, I was certain that I had discovered the source of Brontë's garden scene, a source that enriched the novel and one that contemporary readers would have recognized. Brontë wrote that the garden was "Eden-like," and by substituting the adulterous Rochester for God, she was, I concluded, warning readers against romantic self-deception. Or so I argued until I found out that Miles was born in 1868, twenty years after the publication of *Jane Eyre.* Once such a discovery would have ended all thought of publication. Not now, however, for I have grown more adept with particulars. Since *Jane Eyre* was popular with religious readers, it seemed reasonable to assume that Miles was familiar with the novel. In any case I have recently completed an essay entitled *"Jane Eyre* and 'In the Garden': From Fiction to Song, a Study of Influence."

A friend has urged me not to publish the article, saying that I have done such violence to fact that the article is absurd. My friend is wrong. Whether Miles influenced Brontë or Brontë, Miles, or Miles never heard of *Jane Eyre*, is beside the point. Facts don't matter if my article is momentarily interesting. While looking through a scrapbook this past Christmas, I found a copy of *My Weekly Reader*, "The Children's Magazine." The issue was for the week beginning January 17, 1949, and the lead story was entitled "The Baby Prince." "A little prince is in the news," the article stated. "His name is Prince Charles. He is just a baby. Prince Charles may be the King of England some day. His grandfather is the King now. Princess Elizabeth is the mother of the baby prince. She is proud of her baby." The particulars of the article don't matter. In 1949 the story was about Charles and Elizabeth; recently it concerned William and Diana. While time has changed the names and, as in the case of my article, interpretation has changed facts, the tales told by the *Weekly Reader* and literary criticism remain much the same.

In the less abstract world of a person's life, however, particulars, as Mr. Ligon implied, can matter a great deal. Some years ago I taught in Syria, and when Vicki and I rented an apartment, Ahmad, our landlord, rummaged through a storage bin and found a baby carriage. He presented it to us, saying he hoped we would fill it before we left the country. The carriage remained empty, but the power of suggestion grew full, and shortly after returning home Vicki and I learned that we would be parents. I wrote Ahmad and told him Vicki was going to have a baby. The news surprised him and his family. "All," he wrote back, "are stundered." When I received Ahmad's letter, I wondered what he meant by stundered. At the time I thought the word was simply a misspelling. I now know better. During the four years that have passed since Ahmad wrote, Francis and Edward have been born and I have learned the particulars of being stundered.

Two months ago I entered a cross-country race that followed old logging roads up a small mountain. On the morning of the race, Vicki tried to discourage me. "Only a fool would run this race," she said; "if you break something, don't expect any sympathy from me. I have the children to take care of." I ran carefully and did not fall. When I got home, I felt proud and relieved.

"Vicki," I shouted as I opened the back door; "I survived." And that's the last thing I said for a while. Suddenly one foot shot out and up behind me, and I pitched head first against the coat closet door and then, lurching sideways, fell across a kitchen chair. Edward had left a Matchbox car on the floor in the kitchen. The car was not hurt, but in falling I twisted my ankle. By evening it was bigger than a coconut, and my running season was over. As I lay on the floor, though, I was not upset. I had long since grown accustomed to cuts, bruises, and sleepless nights, all the rough particulars of being stundered.

Not only do particulars help define words like *stundered*, but attention to particulars is necessary in effective writing. This summer I am lecturing in an institute on children's literature sponsored at the University of Connecticut by the National Endowment for the Humanities. Although the institute has received much favorable publicity, some people think children's literature a relatively unimportant study and think the funds allocated for the institute should go instead toward maintaining highways or cleaning up toxic waste. Recently the director of the institute received a postcard from a disgruntled Bridgeport resident. The writer chose his words carefully. "Ga ga—goo goo, Ca ca—poo poo," he wrote, "Stop wasting TAX Bucks!"

Although effective writing depends upon using particulars, living a good life often depends upon avoiding them. Not long ago a friend wrote me from Syria. After graduating from college, he wanted to teach in a university. Since the Ministry of Education had sponsored his undergraduate studies, or as he put it, he had been "internally scholarized," he would not be eligible for a university post until he had spent several years teaching at the secondary school level. My friend's letter was informative, and I read it to a colleague interested in international education. Our new department secretary overheard me, and when I read the phrase "internally scholarized," she asked, "What does that mean? I don't understand."

"What?" I said, light leaping to my eyes; "You are working in an English department, and you have never been scholarized? Ho, ho," I chuckled, "you will learn soon enough." And then I stopped. She was pink-cheeked and round-eyed, only twenty-two and as fresh as milk from a dairy. Once I would have relished explaining the particulars of scholarizing, and if the opportunity had arisen, would have gone an indiscreet step or two farther. Now married, with two, almost three, children, a comfortable house, a reputation as a wholesome family man, and even thinking about going to church again, I was not about to contemplate the particulars of scholarizing.

Success may depend as much upon thwarting requests for particulars as it does upon controlling the urge to offer them. Last year I went to Texas to be interviewed for a university post. I flew from Hartford and changed planes in Atlanta. Although there was quite a bit of time between my arrival and departure from Atlanta, I did not wander around the airport. Instead, as soon as I got off the Hartford plane I hurried to the embarkation area and waited for my next flight. The other passengers, I thought, might be able to tell me something about the university and the town to which I was traveling. At first I was disappointed; the waiting area was filled with soldiers, computer salesmen, and mothers busy with infants and toddlers. Just as I was about to wander off and buy a thriller, sixteen women appeared. Draped with ornaments and shining like Christmas trees, they were members of an investment club. Each month members sent money to New

York, and once a year the members flew to New York to consult with their broker and spend a lively tax-deductible week, buying clothes, going to the theater, and eating in fine restaurants. When I discovered they were from the town to which I was flying, I asked them lots of questions. "It is," one woman said, "an extremely difficult place for outsiders. Few members of the university community ever have the right sort of introduction. Their backgrounds are so different from ours." At this point the person unaccustomed to southern ways might have blurted out the particulars of his pedigree. That would have been a mistake, revealing him to be so underbred as to care for society and also destroying mystery, that rich topsoil in which gossip plants reputation and acceptability. "Oh, there would be no problem for me," I answered gaily, "my mamma would make three phone calls, and I would be all set."

I had avoided the pitfall; my self-assurance left no room to doubt my particulars, and as we boarded the flight, one of the women approached me. "I am," she said, "Mrs. Hill Whelwell; after you are settled, have your wife call me. I would be glad to nominate her for the Junior League and the Docents."

The rule of better judgment, alas, is only sporadic, and it is always a struggle for me to keep my particulars private. This past fall I ran a road race in New London during a storm. The rain fell in stinging sheets, and the wind was so gusty that running a straight course was impossible. Somehow, though, I thrived, and despite being blown about and getting soaking wet and chafed, I ran one of my best races. Near the end I sprinted past three men and two women and felt wonderful. At least I did until I heard one of the women that I passed ask the other, "Was that a man or a woman that finished ahead of us?" I am so slow that taking running seriously is impossible. I am the essential gentleman, for when I run, it is almost always "women and children first." Yet the question irritated me. It is true that I am growing old and have lost my shape, but few people—least of all women, I fumed—confused me with a girl. "If I showed her a couple of particulars," I thought, "then, by God, she'd know what finished in front of her."

Of course I did not show her anything, and if I had, she would not have been intrigued. She was not so young herself, and as people grow older, they lose much of their curiosity and not simply are able but indeed want to avoid particulars. Vicki and I live near Willimantic, a small mill town in eastern Connecticut. Along Main Street are the Hooker Hotel, which rents rooms by the week and the month; the bus station; Bev's cigar stand and fun shop; and offices for army and navy recruiters. We like Willimantic, but the world of the Junior League and Docents is far away. Occasionally Vicki and I used to eat pizza in a restaurant called the Bear Garden. Always smoky and with a bar adjoining the dining room, the Bear Garden was not paradise. We didn't mind, though, because the pizza was good and the hubbub in the bar was too general to disturb us. Then one night a voice rose above the din, and a man shouted, "He can stick his dick in it." Vicki and I looked at each other, momentarily intrigued by *it*. Silently we both decided that we did not want to know more and almost simultaneously said. "Whew, I am full. I have had enough; are you ready to go?"

As a person grows older and becomes less curious about the present, he often becomes more curious about the past. The particulars of the past are safe and comfortable. Rarely do they affect behavior and influence the present or undermine the future. How much better it is to wander through musty barns and attics wondering about lives of the dead than it is to look closely at daily life. Perhaps Vicki is right when she urges me to toughen up. All I know is that thinking about the particulars of such behavior makes me unhappy. Far better for me, and maybe for her too, if I think about the doings of my great-grandfather Daniel Griffin just after the Civil War. While in Georgia in July 1872, he wrote a letter to Nannie Brown, his future wife and my great-grandmother. "I am about to become a politician again (as in the old times of busting up the Union Leagues)," he said. "Some of the best friends I ever had are running for office in this county. I have met several & talked to them of my worst enemies, who made out charges & swore to them, carried them to Atlanta & got the Yankees after me, but its allright *I have no feeling against them whatsoever.* It makes me feel strange to be that way. I must certainly have retrograded, lost all spirit but I don't care." What Griffin cared about was Nannie, back in Tennessee, and he was on his best behavior. In the past his spirit had gotten him shot and run out of Georgia. But what exactly had he done? I wondered, as I read his letters. He was a prickly man, quick to take offense, so cantankerous that he eventually left Tennessee for Texas. But what, I thought, had he done to get the Yankees after him?

While the present tore a rough path through the Bear Garden, I read old letters, trying to discover the particulars of Griffin's past. Last year, though, my old Pontiac broke down for the last time, and buying a new car forced me out of the attic and the past and thrust me into the present. A friend suggested the Mazda, and until I visited the dealer in Manchester, I considered it seriously. "Yeah, we've got some," the dealer said. "I'll be with you in a minute." Then, clearing his throat, he leaned across his desk and spat heavily into the lower left-hand drawer. After that sight no options could have made the Mazda appealing, and I left without looking at the car. Returning home, I went to the attic and began rummaging through scrapbooks. In one was a letter sent to me by my grandfather in 1945. When I carried it downstairs to show to Vicki, I had forgotten about cars and the crude particulars of the present. "I am thinking about dashing down to Nashville," grandfather wrote, "the fireman here in Richmond promised to loan me a wagon and engine, and boy when I hit the road, look out for I'll be coming round the corner when I come." Like grandfather's letter, marvelous things have come into my life from corners of attics. Not long ago I found a muzzle-loading rifle. Attached to the stock were two silver feet; from toe to heel each foot was three inches long. On one was engraved "T.D.

MUTTER MD Presented by W. Robinson." On the barrel was the name of the gunsmith, "Robinson of Philadelphia." Dr. Mutter, it seems, must have cured Robinson of some persistent, if not terrible, foot ailment, in appreciation of which Robinson made the gun. But what, I wondered, were the particulars of Robinson's ailment? Since finding the gun, I have spent several enjoyable hours in a library, reading about foot problems, and although I have no idea what bothered Robinson, I do know some curious things about Charcot's joint, Cotton's fracture, snail nail, trigger toe, and hallux valgus.

For several years I lived in Hanover, New Hampshire. In 1978 I moved to Connecticut and until this spring had not returned to New Hampshire. In February, though, I went to Hanover to discuss publication of a book. After meeting with an editor, I ate lunch and started back to my car to drive home. Leaving so abruptly struck me, however, as sad; after living in a town eight years, there ought to be someone, I thought, whom I would like to see, and instead of driving straight back to Connecticut, I drove to the apartment building in which I used to live. Across the hall from me had lived Mrs. Moore, an elderly widow. Over the years we had become friends, having tea and gossiping together at least twice a week. For two years after I left Hanover, I sent Mrs. Moore Christmas and birthday cards, but then the correspondence stopped when I went abroad. When I parked behind the building, I had no idea if Mrs. Moore was still alive. Her apartment, though, was on the ground floor, and if she was still there, the windows, I knew, would be full of African violets.

I hoped she was alive. The thought that seven years' absence could erase all traces of my presence in a place made me melancholy, and when I looked through her window and saw pot after pot of bright purple violets, my spirits rose. Nothing seemed to have changed inside Mrs. Moore's apartment. Old newspapers were still strewn on the floor around her second best sofa; on the wall was a painting of a covered bridge, as orange and garish as I remembered. Mr. Moore's picture was on the same place on the bookshelf, and by Mrs. Moore's footstool was a pair of slippers just like the ones she had been wearing when I moved away. Even the topics of conversation were the same: Skidmore and Dartmouth reunions, her grandson Kevin, and her two boyfriends, both of whom were now in their eighties but who were as eager to marry her as they had been in 1978.

"Nothing," I said, as I stood up to leave, "nothing seems to have changed since I was here."

"Oh, dear," she said, "there have been changes"; and, taking me by the hand, she led me into the hall. "This place is different," she said. To me nothing seemed changed. Although the walls were white, the stairwell remained dark and gloomy. Outside Mrs. Moore's door was the same coffee table; on it was a familiar wicker basket. In the basket was *The Valley News,* which the paperboy put there every afternoon at three o'clock.

"I can't see any changes," I said.

"You should pay more attention to particulars," she answered and, pointing to the ceiling, said, "That's new." On the ceiling was a round, cream-colored smoke detector. "It," she explained, "was put there two years ago. You must learn to be alert if you want to succeed in life," she continued. "Did I ever tell you about the man my Grace married? At first he seemed fine. But once we got to know him, we learned better."

Too Late

Sister Sue, Uncle Andrew, and their nephew Little Henry lived on a small farm outside Shelbyville, Tennessee. Uncle Andrew had a big garden, Sister Sue made their clothes, and the family, so the story goes, was almost self-sufficient. About every six weeks, though, Sue told Andrew to hitch up the wagon, and they all set out for Shelbyville and shopping. Sue would have enjoyed going to town more often; unfortunately, Andrew was addicted to alcohol, and whenever he went to Shelbyville, chances were good he would misbehave. In the hope of finishing her shopping before Andrew was incapacitated, Sue had learned to race through stores. For his part, Andrew had also learned a thing or two, and as soon as he dropped Sue and Little Henry off at McClure's, he lit out for the back room of Campbell's Barber Shop.

On this particular Saturday, Sue did not have much shopping to do. She looked at camisoles that had just arrived from Philadelphia, examined bolts of cloth, and bought a churn at the hardware store. By two o'clock she had finished, and as she stepped out of Mr. Simpson's Hardware, she turned to Little Henry and said, "Run over to Mr. Campbell's and give Uncle Andrew this message. Tell him that I am through shopping, and if he is not too drunk, it's time for him to hitch up the horse and drive us home."

Henry hurried over to Campbell's and found Andrew warmly ensconced in the back room. "Uncle Andrew," he said, "Sister Sue sent me with a message for you."

"What is it, Little Henry?" Andrew answered.

"She said," Henry replied, "that if you weren't too drunk, you were to hitch up the horse and drive us home."

"Tell Sister Sue," Andrew said, pausing for breath and drink, "tell Sister Sue that the message came too late."

Messages are forever reaching me too late. Not long ago, I was asked to read the publications of a man who taught in a western university and then make a recommendation about the man's tenure. I agreed to do so, and two weeks later a big box arrived, crammed with books and articles. Accompanying the box was a letter saying that I need not return the books. I have three small children, and my house looks like a landfill. The children are as acquisitive as hamsters and have stuffed every cranny with toys. As their possessions have increased, mine have decreased, and what was once my library is now their playroom. Only a few books remain on the shelves, and there is not space for more. As soon as I finished reading the man's publications, I threw them away. Eight days after I wrote my report, I received a letter from the chairman of the department in which the man taught. He was "extremely embarrassed," the chairman said, "to have to request" the return of one of the books. "I did not realize when we sent the material that we had borrowed copies of this book from professors and the University Library." He was away, he continued, when the books were brought in "and so did not realize that we were sending out a very valuable edition."

"The message," I wrote back without hesitation, "came too late," and I advised the chairman "to promote the man and promote him fast."

For Uncle Andrew receiving a message early was sobering. Similarly, getting a message late often brings pleasure. Ron, my roommate in graduate school, was a square-shouldered, crew-cut Canadian from Winnipeg, a man so straightforward that he could not tell a lie, much less imagine someone stretching the truth for fun. Because Ron was so forthright, people about him often bent facts and played jokes on him. In Princeton there were many black squirrels, and since neither Ron nor I had ever seen black squirrels before, we occasionally speculated about their ancestry. One day while Ron was studying at his desk, I burst into the room. "Ron," I shouted, "go downstairs quickly; there is a squat in the courtyard."

"A what?" he said, looking up from his book and turning around.

"A squat, a squat," I yelled; "these black squirrels are really different. Sometimes they mate with cats, and the offspring are called squats. Get your camera," I added, "there are not many of them."

"Wow," he said, rushing over to the dresser and jerking his camera out of the top drawer. "What do they look like?"

"They have cats' heads but eat nuts and live in trees," I answered; "hurry before this one disappears."

"Wow," Ron said again, shouting as he ran thumping down the stairs, "wait till folks in Winnipeg hear about this."

If a person understands too quickly, he can miss sustenance as well as sustaining laughter. When I was small, I had a pet rooster named Sammy. Sammy was a one-man bird with a strong distrust of the human female. When Sherry, my cousin, scattered corn in his path, he was wary. Cocking his head, he watched her carefully; then when she turned away, he flew at her, scolding and clawing. Sherry screamed, dropped the pan of corn, and ran crying to the house. I thought Sammy's performance fine and wanted an encore. Earlier Sherry had dumped a bucket of green bugs on me as I sat in my sandbox. Unfortunately I was the only one who applauded Sammy's misogyny. That night we had fried chicken for dinner. Halfway through a drumstick, I bit into the truth. "Is this Sammy Rooster?" I asked.

"Yes," my grandfather answered, and I started to cry.

Happily, however, the message had come too late to ruin the meal. Before tears started to flow, I smelled the chicken in my hand. Sammy had never been so sweet. My eyes dried; my mouth watered; and, reaching across the table, I grabbed the breast and said, "He was my pet and I can have what I want."

Familiarity can stifle curiosity. Because they are far away and cannot be seen clearly, distant objects often appeal to the imagination. In a similar fashion, acquaintances or family members who are distant in time or place frequently become objects of speculation and sources of pleasure. Possessions of family members whom I have never seen fill my house. Born too late to know them, I look at their things and spend happy hours wondering through their days. In a rolltop desk in a storeroom, I recently found a box of silver souvenir spoons. Turning them over in my hands, I speculated about the person who owned them. Perhaps they belonged to a young girl who at the turn of the century traded with her friends for them, much as I traded baseball cards in the 1950s. Which was worth more, I asked myself, a spoon in the bowl of which appeared "Parthenon Tennessee Centennial" and a meticulous engraving of the replica of the Parthenon in Nashville or a spoon depicting the School for the Deaf in Council Bluffs, Iowa? Celebrating Tennessee's centennial in 1897, the first spoon was carefully done, while the engraving of the school, four stories high with ninety windows, was a hurried, a slapdash affair, jammed into the bowl and almost dripping over the rim. Still, spoons celebrating the centennial must have been common, while those depicting the School for the Deaf were probably comparatively rare. Could one trade, I thought, a crude "Soldier's & Sailor's Home" in Grand Island, Nebraska, for an ornate engraving of St. Louis's "Festival Hall & Cascade Gardens," complete with lake, fountains. and gondolas? Probably the Soldier's & Sailor's Home wasn't enough, and one would have to sweeten the trade with a spoon depicting the "Nature Cabin" in Asheville, North Carolina, on the stem of which were green enameled leaves and a posy of blue violets.

Maybe, though, I have things wrong. Instead of being children's playthings, the spoons belonged to a married couple who purchased them whenever they went on a trip. Perhaps they traveled through Iowa and Nebraska on their honeymoon, ending in Seattle, where they bought a spoon depicting the waterfront. In front was a tugboat; behind loomed a steamship; behind that, standing against a gray sky like a forest of bare limbs in winter, were the masts and tangled riggings of sailing ships. On a later trip the couple may have gone to Atlantic City; and on June 20, 1901, for that was the date engraved on the spoon, they stood under the lighthouse. I like to think of them there, holding hands while the beam spun above them like a sun. I like to imagine them buying a spoon so that they would have something to remind them of youth and love as they grew old together. Perhaps, though, they never grew old and instead died young. The box contained no spoons dated after 1904. Indeed, the only spoon from 1904 had a picture of the Tampa Bay Hotel in the bowl. The spoon was bright and cheerful. In the enamel on the stem were white blossoms, two oranges, and a wreath of green leaves. Maybe the husband became ill; the couple went to Florida for his health and in a burst of hope bought the spoon, vibrant with color and the promise of a future. Of course I will never know; born too late, I can only imagine.

Today is the twelfth of December 1985. In the desk I also found a letter to Santa Claus "mailed" a hundred years ago, on December 12, 1885, from Bellevue, Tennessee. "Dear Santa Claus," the letter began, "You are such a nice old man that I hate to ask you for many things but I hope you can bring me a Doll (china Doll) and an Orange, some Candy and Nuts, some Raisins and some fire Crackers. You may not remember me but I am the liveliest little girl in these woods. I am the Belle of three. You may bring me a Candy Dog, and a Ring Cup and Saucer and Plate.

Please dont forget me for I would be greatly disappointed. Affectionately your little Girl, Lulie Griffin." My great-aunt Lula died when I was young, and I know little about her. I do know that eventually she got a doll of sorts, an only son, fragile and remarkably talented. At twenty he broke down, and when he was confined to an institution, Aunt Lula's happiness shattered like china dropped on a sidewalk. Now as I read Lulie's letter, I think of my three dolls and Christmas, and I am frightened. Would that I had not found Lulie's letter. I knew too much to create a happy life for her. Knowledge of what the years brought the liveliest little girl in the woods hangs over my Christmas, and when Francis and Edward come to me to ask about Santa Claus, I want to wrap my arms around them and say, "Santa will always bring you"—and then, in a lower tone, "me"—"whatever you want."

Being a nick too late can be more invigorating than being in the nick of time. Last week was dull. I graded term papers and changed diapers. In between I watched television. Vicki cooked, cleaned, and drove, and the days fell silently away. Then one morning while I was at my desk and Vicki was at nursery school with Francis, I heard the downstairs toilet flush. Almost asleep and thinking only about grades, I half-heard the sound. When I suddenly realized that only Edward and Eliza were home, neither of whom was housebroken, I ran into the bathroom. There stood Edward, his hand on the handle of the toilet, while Eliza clutched the edge of the bowl and, leaning over, peered intently inside. I reached the toilet in time to see a wooden block swing around once and then disappear down the drain. The only letter visible on the block was a red P, the abbreviation, I was certain, for plumber. Being late awakened me. Not once during the rest of the day did I doze at my desk. While keeping a water ear cocked for gurgling, I graded all my papers, something I would not have accomplished if I had fished the block out before it disappeared.

A dinner party missed is frequently the subject of more conversation than one attended. When a letter which looks like an invitation arrives in the mail, I let it sit on the kitchen table for at least two days before opening it. I will do almost anything to avoid the after-dinner-party, early-morning coffee hangover that keeps one's eyes open and stuck to the television while his brain twists and turns and tosses thought this way and that in a futile attempt to sleep. What I like is the invitation that arrives too late, particularly the invitation that purposely has been sent too late. In such invitations is the creamy stuff of conversation, full-bodied and more stimulating than any mug of Columbian brew.

Twenty years ago Hugh Broster was one of my best friends at Cambridge University. Boisterous and hardy, he rowed every afternoon. Never seeming to tire, he pulled his oar just as strongly at the end of a workout as at the beginning. In the evenings he drank deep, and many times we plunged into our cups, surfacing to career along Silver Street, breaking the dark with laughter and song. After I left Cambridge, Hugh wrote me. He said he had taken a job in London and urged me to look him up if ever I was in town. In 1975 I went to London to work on a book. One day I picked up a telephone directory, found Hugh's name, and called him. Over the phone he sounded like the same hearty fellow I remembered. He said he had recently married and was packing to move into a new flat; otherwise, he would invite me and my wife to dinner.

"Never mind," I said, "you eat with us."

"That sounds super," he answered, and we set a date for the following week.

The afternoon of the dinner I bought a bottle of Scotch, and as soon as Hugh stepped out of the car outside my house, I handed him a stiff one. "How extraordinarily nice," he said; "here's to us." Since Hugh was always fast out of the glass, I had gotten a little start on him; otherwise I might have noticed a frown on his wife's face. Still, I didn't notice, and within a short time Hugh had plopped down comfortably on our couch and was nearing the five-eighths pole of his second Scotch. Sipping orange juice and sitting in a hard, stiff-backed armchair, his wife didn't even touch the wine I had bought for dinner. Nevertheless she seemed affectionate. When Hugh started galloping through his fourth drink, she rose out of the chair, went to the couch, sat down, and taking the glass out of his hand and putting it on the coffee table, clasped both his hands in hers.

"By God," Hugh roared, "Dorcas is affectionate. What a wife! You'll never guess where I met her, Sam."

"Where?" I asked.

"Just a minute, babe," Hugh said, turning to Dorcas, "you are holding me too tight; I can't get to my drink." After freeing his right hand and jockeying back along the rail, Hugh told me where he met her. "At an evangelical retreat—can you believe it? Me of all people at a church retreat," he said, adding, "and here's something you really won't believe. Tonight is the first time I have had a drink since we were married." Looking at Dorcas, I had no trouble believing Hugh. Distaste given way to condemnation, and she fixed us with a stare that would have made the stoutest son of Belial flinch. Would that I had been able to do something. Unfortunately, Hugh and I were thundering along; alcohol had its whip hand up, and neither of us was about to pull up short. The best Dorcas could hope for was a breakdown, and that didn't happen. In a cloud of remembrance we pounded through story into song. Midnight came, and Hugh didn't want to leave. "Best time I have had," he said, "since my wedding night." When we eventually steered him to the car, he gave Dorcas the keys, "something you will have to do, Sam," he said to me, "when you eat with us. How about it, Dorcas old thing, how about Sambo's coming for dinner on the twenty-fourth?"

"Hugh," she answered, "I don't think we will be unpacked by then."

"Well, what about the thirty-first?" he said. This date, too, wasn't right, and after Hugh suggested four more, all of which Dorcas found unsuitable, he gave up, saying, "Bloody Hell, we will have to work something out at home. When are you going back to America, Sam?" When I told him we would not leave until the end of June, six months away, he shouted, "Terrific!"

and declared, "We will be able to have a lot of fun before you go." With that, he slapped Dorcas on the bottom and saying, "Slip that thing in gear, love; let's go home," got into the car and fell asleep. Six months passed without my hearing from Hugh. In July we flew home; in September school started; in November I received a letter from Hugh. It had been sent to our London address and then forwarded. In the letter Hugh invited us to set a date for dinner; he apologized for not inviting us sooner but explained that settling into the new flat had taken more time than either he or Dorcas had foreseen. "After that wonderful evening we spent with you," he wrote, "Dorcas didn't want you to visit until everything was perfect." The letter was dated 6 May. Alas, Hugh must have put the letter into a coat pocket and forgotten about it; the postmark on the envelope was a bit later, August 29 to be exact. The message had come too late, so late that it gave me great pleasure, more pleasure than I would have had sipping orange juice with the elect. I immediately wrote Hugh, criticizing the British mail service for not delivering the letter in May and saying we were sorry not to have seen more of him and his bride during our stay. "Never mind, though," I ended, "I do a lot of writing, and we will return. When we get to London, the first thing we will do is get in touch. I can't name a day, but it could be tomorrow. Tell Dorcas to expect me on the other end of the line whenever she answers the telephone."

Since writing Hugh, I have been in London several times, but I have not telephoned him. It is too late in life for me to get up to bad, although, to be honest, I am occasionally tempted to cavort. Two years ago I attended a literary conference in Dallas. I was on my best behavior and drank ginger ale and ate a small dinner. At ten o'clock my lights were out, and I was pulling the covers over my shoulders when I heard a conversation outside my door.

"Why don't you come to my room and have a little bourbon," he said.

"I'd love to," she answered.

Like Venus splashing out of the sea, I rose shaking from the sheets. Unlike the goddess of love, however, I have lost my figure. Distant parts have become acquainted as my chest has fallen and my thighs have risen. When I unbuttoned the top of my pajamas, I looked into the mirror. For the youthful, the evening was young; for me it was too late. I buttoned my pajamas back up and turning on the television, crawled into bed and watched reruns of "Ozzie and Harriet."

In life a person will be late many times. Opportunities will narrowly be missed, and although one may feel regret, the regret soon passes. Most things that seem momentarily important are usually insignificant. About the only thing the aging man regrets being too late for is the company of young women. "If I had only met her twenty years ago" repeats itself, scratching the mind like a needle hung in a groove on a record. Age may change from forty to forty-five to fifty-five, but the needle stays caught and the words never wear away. I first heard them twelve years ago when I was teaching in Jordan. My classes were filled with girls, girls whose eyes were as brown and as rich and sweetly promising as a box of chocolate truffles. One day I mentioned that I was going to spend the evening scrubbing my kitchen floor.

"Oh, professor," a girl said to me after class, "I wish I could wash your floors."

"So do I," I thought and leaping far beyond bucket and soap imagined the life we could have shared if I had not been too old.

Believing that life would be better if one were not too late is a fiction. Last week a former student came by my office. Some years ago she wrote poetry that at the time made me regret being too late for her. Since graduating from college, though, she had left poetry as well as a husband and two jobs behind. Now she was working on her master's in business administration, so she could, as she put it, "get into the big bucks." Years had not treated her kindly, and the full, soft, nougatlike roundness that I remembered had dried, cracked, and split into sharp, stale splinters. Conversation was difficult; nothing flowed, and as idea after idea caught and tore on her edges, I found myself thinking, "Thank goodness I was too late." And that's the way I want things to stay. Because I am usually too late, life has treated me gently. I have not gotten what I deserve, and Vicki and I have slipped along, slowly building a marriage out of the mortar and solid brick of experience, not the insubstantial candy of dream.

I am on time for many things; sometimes I am even early. Would that the morning robin got the earthworm or even the warmth that appearing at midday brings. Strands of the fabric of lies we think beneficial to children, maxims have little to do with actual life. Hopping about in the cold, the early bird rarely sips orange juice and sits down to a leisurely breakfast of hot buttered biscuits and fat, steaming patties of country sausage. While the early bird shivers in the damp, the successful birds among us are still abed, comfortably buried under eiderdowns and dreaming of bright-eyed little chickadees. Instead of admiring the early bird, they hold him in contempt, seeing him, if they notice him at all, as an emblem not of industry but of silly, bedraggled failure. To appear early is to appear absurd. I live close to the University of Connecticut and walk to class or any meetings I have to attend. This past spring on what I thought was graduation day, I got up early and dressed meticulously. Fixing the mortarboard hat with its gold tassel securely and scenically on my head and draping my orange-and-black hood and black robe over my shoulders so they would flow grandly, I swept out the door. As I strode across campus, people looked at me oddly. I thought nothing about it; people always stare when I wear academic paraphernalia. In truth, I enjoy the attention. Tossing back my head, I lock my jaw and pace firmly and haughtily along, a being, my step implies, from an elevated world, a creature so far above trifles that no one dares trifle with him. Not until I arrived at the auditorium where graduation was held did I notice that I was alone. No parents, no students, and no professors clustered about. The only person in sight was a campus policeman.

"My good man," I said, "has graduation been moved to another less scenic location?"

"No sir," he answered, "it's right here"—and then he stopped for a second—"right here, next Saturday."

Two years ago a policeman and I had an informative discussion about Joseph Mitchell, the old *New Yorker* writer. Mitchell is a good writer; comparatively few people know about him today, though, and the discussion I had with the policeman was enjoyable. The talk, however, would not have occurred if I had not tried to renew my driver's license fourteen months after it expired. Although I have never had an unpleasant conversation with a policeman, I rarely talk to the police. They make me nervous; I am always frightened they will find me out. About what remains vague, but I suspect there is something they could uncover. As a result I have paid careful attention to matters automotive for the past two years. Two months ago I noticed that the sticker on my license plate read "Dec 86." "Vicki," I said yesterday morning; "I am going to renew the license today. If I don't do it now, I might forget and get caught out like two years ago." Accordingly, after breakfast I wrote a check to the state for the fee, gathered the necessary papers—emissions-test certificate, registration, and insurance forms—and drove to the Department of Motor Vehicles in Willimantic. The line at the counter didn't bother me. As I watched people fumbling about for forms they forgot to bring, I felt confident and superior. "When old Sam gets up early," I thought, "the worms better look out." When my turn came, I handed my papers to the clerk and said, "Santa has harnessed Rudolph and is beating the Christmas rush this year." The clerk started to process the papers, but unaccountably she stopped, examined the registration, and then turned back to me.

"You have beat the rush all right, Rudolph. This is 1985; the license for your sleigh doesn't expire until 1986. Santa doesn't need you this year," she added, as my face reddened, "you just trot along home and come back next Christmas."

Being late leads to more than freedom from embarrassment. Not only does being behind the times undermine the tendency toward pretentiousness, but it helps sustain intellectual integrity.

Like the wash behind a big wave, cultural trends can pull a strong person under. For years I have struggled to lag behind the times. I haven't read a newspaper for a decade, and recently I have stopped watching news on television. While acquaintances dash off to cultural hot spots and splash about in fashionable thought, I have stayed home, thinking about the little things with which I am most familiar: childhood, school, and family. By remaining apart from trends, I hope to dig closer to truth. The digging is not easy; although a vein occasionally glitters before me, I have yet to strike a mother lode and am often tempted to toss my pick aside and head for the beach. Recently an agent wrote me. "Tales about life in the country are in," he wrote, "and you are just a good old country boy. Why don't you write a novel about the country and cash in?" Although I know a few country stories and as a child spent happy summers on my grandfather's farm in Virginia, I was brought up in the city, went to private schools, and danced with debutantes. Any extended piece I wrote about rural life would ring false, money or no. "Country, my behind," I responded; "country club boy would be more like it."

I am not bothered when I hear people discussing things about which I know little. My father, however, became so chagrined by what he calls my "know-nothing-about-the-present attitude" that for Christmas last year he gave me a subscription to *Time* magazine. When the magazine arrives, I put it on the kitchen table beside the dinner invitations, and if the children don't immediately slice it up for a collage, I leaf through it. Although I occasionally learn something, not much in the magazine sticks to my ribs. Politicians promise peace, and wars break out. Celebrities prance around half naked, and World Series bounces into World Series. Still, I am not completely at ease about being dissociated from trends. Being late suits me, but I worry about the effects such an attitude will have upon my children. A cousin is having his two-year-old son tutored so the boy will be admitted to a nursery school for the gifted. "If the boy is so damn gifted," I said to Vicki when she told me, "why does he have to be tutored? This is the silliest thing I have ever heard of. The boy would be better off in the woods with Francis and Edward catching bugs."

In part my reaction was strong because I feel guilty about not pushing my children. Am I, I often wonder, condemning them to mediocrity? Life in contemporary society, *Time* tells me, is highly competitive. Should my boys be tied to a schedule like their cousin, studying French at two? When an acquaintance told me that his four-year-old daughter recently informed him that not only does she intend to be a brain surgeon but she is determined to focus her studies on the thalamus, suddenly the single hope I had for my children—that they would become decent people, wise enough to be satisfied with ordinary fare—seemed limited and threateningly restrictive. My boys would be out of place in a nursery school of aspiring brain surgeons and theoretical physicists. At four and a half, Francis wants to be a detective, not an Adam Dalgleish or a Hercule Poirot, but a member of the Bloodhound Gang, a group of children who solve mysteries on "3-2-1 Contact," a television show that comes on right after "Mr. Rogers' Neighborhood" and just before dinner. For his part, Edward, who is two and a half, is not so ambitious and wants to be a boogyman, so, as he says, he can hide in the dark and "scare the poop out of people."

Characters like the Boogyman live in my house. Tommy Raw-Head lurks under the basement stairs; Bloody Bones stomps about in the attic, sniffing for the blood of Englishmen and little visitors. The Wallpaper Wolf, Mess Monster, and Black Annis, a bearded hag with fingers sharper than nails, drop in and take up residence in closets when the boys misbehave. From what Vicki tells me, few homes today are hospitable to such creatures. Computers and creative toys have driven them out into the killing sunlight. Alas, my children play with blocks, stuffed animals, and crayons, and I don't know anything about computers. For that matter I can hardly type; I am such a poor typist that I cannot use an electric typewriter. What will happen when my boys go to school and run up against all those children programmed to perform, and to win? Maybe "it" is already too late for Francis and Edward. Actually that might be good. Always too late, perhaps they won't wax ambitious and set timetables for themselves. Instead of plotting the future, maybe they will learn to enjoy the present, and then wonder about the past. Ultimately living smashes all timetables into kindling. Instead of climbing to cold heights, how much better to stretch out before a fire and read a book, not a book about the future but about the past, a book like the one I just finished, A. J. Liebling's *Back Where I Came From*. My edition was published in 1938. In it I found a piece of yellow paper on which was written "Milk, Cream, and Sweetcrackers." The list is almost poetic—"Milk, Cream, and Sweetcrackers." Since I don't know who drew the list up, I have spent a warm hour tasting Sweetcrackers and thinking about the author and messages that come too late.

Loose Ends

Matty and Tom, so the tale goes, had been
sweethearts since sixth grade, and everybody in Red Boiling
Springs expected them to marry. There was little in Red Boiling
Springs to disrupt the bright, babbling course of true love. Since
the end of the nineteenth century when sick people began to
neglect the wells and turn instead to doctors and hospitals, and
when families sought summer pleasures farther afield, on
beaches in Florida or North Carolina and not on the porches of
the Grand Hotel or around "Ma" Fentress's table, Red Boiling
Springs had dozed lazily. Out of habit each summer a few oc-
togenarians took the train up from Nashville to drink the waters:
Red Heaven, Yellow Bird, and for those who over long years had
lost their senses of smell and taste, the powerful Black Twist. In
April Mr. Hawes opened the first floor of the Grand; in May, the
second; and in July, if business looked promising, which it rarely
did, he opened the third. The top two floors remained shut all
summer, a home for squirrels and mice and an occasional barn
owl. Unlike earlier times when the streets were sprinkled morning and afternoon to keep down the dust from carriages, almost

nothing moved. From the porch of the Grand came the sleepy sound of rockers slipping across loose boards and the occasional sputter of a dry cough. Noon could just as well have been midnight, things were so quiet. At least they were quiet until TVA and the dam builders came to town.

Almost overnight cars and trucks clogged Main Street. Willie Garthright turned his tobacco field into a parking lot and rented space by the month. Mr. Hawes opened the top floors of the Grand and over the front door hung a string of gold lights which spelled HOTEL. Ma Fentress's daughter Caroline opened the High Waters Restaurant; not to be outdone, her cousin Comfort started Fields Afloat Cafe. Boulders of business and bustle tumbled through the quiet stream of town life, tearing people from their moorings and sweeping them out of settled channels of living. For a time Matty and Tom went along as before, with eyes and hearts only for each other. But then Denby Mair, an expensively educated engineer from Philadelphia, moved into the Grand. Mair was young and lonely, and Matty was pretty. In comparison to Mair, Tom seemed roughhewn, and it wasn't long before Tom's plans were washed away like the farms behind the dam in the valley.

The town had little sympathy for Tom. Most people were proud that one of their girls had captured the heart of so learned a man, and they turned out in force for the wedding reception at the Grand. As was customary, Mair made a speech. The occasion demanded poetry, and he waxed eloquent. "When I first arrived in Red Boiling Springs," he began, "I was unhappy. I missed the bright lights of the city. The longer I stayed, though, the closer I seemed to be to heaven. One day as I looked about me, the fields shined with flowers the colors of the rainbow. In the distance birds sang like harps; suddenly as I stared into the blue sky a bird of paradise flew towards me. As the bird fluttered above my head chirping sweetly, the air was filled with perfume. Reaching up I took the bird in my arms and drew dear Matty to my breast." Mair's speech struck the right note, and people remarked that

Matty was lucky to marry such a sensitive man. Congratulations and toasts followed the groom's speech.

After some time Tom addressed the couple. "I know exactly what the happy groom means when he compares Red Boiling Springs to heaven," he began; "like him I was once in a field where the flowers appeared bright as the rainbow. I, too, heard music and smelled perfume. When I looked into the sky, I also saw the bird of paradise. Unfortunately I was too slow, and when I reached up to grab the bird, it fluttered its wings and slipped out of my hands. And all I got," Tom concluded, "was a few pieces of tail."

Tom may have been fortunate. Getting part of something is often better than getting all of it. When things are held firmly, they can quickly become ordinary and lose their attraction. Understanding, or grasping things mentally, often leads to their being categorized and filed away on some brown shelf in the mind. In contrast, misunderstandings can be memorable. While students who provide right answers soon sink into the undistinguished mulch of university life, those who get things wrong, who grasp only a piece of an assignment, provide the stuff of fond memory. After I lectured on Rudyard Kipling's *Kim*, Sarah raised her hand. "Mr. Pickering," she began in a voice that sounded remarkably like the trilling of a bird of paradise, "Mr. Pickering, I really enjoyed this book, but I have a question. Why," she continued, "are all the characters members of the same family?"

"What," I said, "what family do you mean?"

"It is this S-A-H-I-B family," she answered, spelling the name out carefully.

Sarah's question livened up a lecture and then a day that was routine. Life easily falls into patterns and is soon a fabric, the loose ends of which are tightly bound together. Strangely enough, it is those loose ends that refuse to bind, the frustrations and failures, that may keep people alive. In trying to pull them out of existence, we grow alert. In Carthage, Tennessee, a little town just down the road from Red Boiling Springs, Mr. Reams Suddaby sold Ford automobiles. A drab, practically inert man, Suddaby spent his days sitting on a bench outside Wigg's barber shop. Not even a customer could get him up. If somebody wanted to look at a car, Suddaby handed him the keys to his garage and told him to "poke around." Only the Ford distributor in Louisville broke the calm of Suddaby's day. Fords were popular, and distributors forced dealers to take cars they didn't want. Although Suddaby rarely left Wigg's bench, his fights with the distributor were famous in Carthage. "This is hilly country. Don't send us any more tractors," Mr. Hawes once heard him yell into the telephone, "and for God's sakes don't send us a Lincoln." Happily, the distributor did not listen, and Suddaby became a man with a grievance. Instead of drying and splitting like Wigg's bench, he became a character; at mention of the word *distributor*, he would rise from the bench like flame, full of color and heat.

As a child I suspected that order was an enemy of life. I liked finding buttons and pins under sofas and behind dressers. I became uncomfortable whenever Mother polished brass and silver for a party. Formality forced toys into bedroom closets and me into a gray suit, and I longed for dusty rooms in which rugs rolled forward across the floor and then ebbed back in bunches like waves, rooms in which ancestors hung tilting on walls, no longer straight and unyielding but with characters as askew as their portraits. The settled, formal house smacked of death, and before parties I often unraveled things. Cicadas, or locusts as I knew them as a boy, fascinated me. I spent summer evenings lying on the grass, catching them as they dug their way up through the soil and crawled toward trees. In my room I kept a stump; on it I put the locusts, and through many nights I sat watching them work out of their shells, first appearing silver, then turning light green, and finally black as their wings unfolded and then hardened like taut sails. In my desk was a cigar box full of locust shells, and often before Mother's guests arrived, I wandered through the house, sticking shells on plants, the backs of curtains, the undersides of chair arms—wherever they were likely to startle.

Snakes were even more effective than bugs in unraveling formality. One Christmas Mother planned a large family dinner. Bertha and Pauline, two cooks who had once worked for us, came to our house late Christmas Eve, one to serve and the other to put the final touches on the meal. After they appeared and before the guests arrived, Mother and Father went to a neighbor's house for a quick cup of Christmas cheer. Wrapped in a gray suit and decorated with a necktie, I stayed home with nothing to do. Before me stretched an evening during which I would sit straight, would not swing my legs, and would endlessly say, "Yes, ma'am; no, ma'am; yes, sir; no, sir."

Then Pauline spoke, "Mister Sammy, do you still catch snakes like you used to?"

Bright, happy chaos suddenly dawned before me. "Oh, yes, Pauline," I answered, "down in the basement I've got the biggest copperhead you ever saw. Let me go get him."

Before Pauline could answer, I ran down the basement stairs and crammed some old newspaper and a piece of wood into a washtub. "I've got him, Pauline," I hollered and started back upstairs. The basement was dark; the only light was behind me near the furnace, and the stairs themselves curved. Consequently people looking down from the kitchen could not distinguish much. Pauline and Bertha stood at the top of the stairs, leaning forward and peering apprehensively into the dark. As I drew close, I made more noise and they seemed to shrink. As soon as I was sure they saw me, I shouted, "Look here, Bertha!" Simultaneously I began to beat the stick about in the paper. The noise sounded like a big snake thrashing about.

"Oh, Lordy," I abruptly yelled, "he's getting loose. I can't hold him. Here Pauline," I screamed, "you take him." And with that, hollering as loudly as I could, I gave the paper an almighty beating and then tossed the tub up the stairs.

"Jesus!" Bertha screamed and slammed the basement door. By the time I got it open, Bertha and Pauline were in the back yard, and that is where they stayed until Mother and Father came home. So many ends were loose that dinner was late. The men seized the occasion to have more drinks than usual. Even some of the women drank more eggnog than they did customarily. Formality unraveled into hearty informality and Christmas cheer, rudely green, embarrassingly red, and wondrously alive.

As one grows older, order becomes increasingly attractive. Nursery school, kindergarten, broken dishwashers, and tree surgeons force a person to organize daily, then weekly and yearly life. Resembling oriental rugs in their ornate designs, schedules are crafted. As friends' lives unravel into failure and death, one decorates his house, keeping it neat and tidy, almost as an attempt to reassure himself that he controls his life. Even so, loose ends remain alluring; strangely enough, they are often woven into the fabric of formality itself, becoming visible reminders of the pleasures of disruption. No longer do I frighten people with snakes and store locust shells in the upper right-hand drawer of my desk; yet I frequently think fondly about the time when I did. I have such thoughts because hanging on the wall in my downstairs bathroom is a print of three cicadas. Published in London on July 12, 1792, by "F. P. Nodder of No. 15 Brewer Street," the print is yellow and brown. Its lines are delicately drawn, and it seems almost Chinese. Still, delicacy has nothing to do with the presence of the print. It hangs in the bathroom because I stuck locust shells on furniture thirty-five years ago. Similarly in the living room over an old sofa, on which family story has it that J. E. B. Stuart, the Confederate general, used to nap, are two prints of snakes: *The Horned Viper,* and *The Secreted Viper and Cobra de Capello,* published in London by J. Wilkes in 1802.

People resist being forced into patterns. Just when I think I have classified a person and filed him safely away, he does something disruptive. Having one's judgments disturbed is rarely pleasant, and this may be why as we grow older we pare acquaintances and resist making new ones. Until recently I thought I knew my neighbor. She appeared to be a generous older soul, the sort who baked carrot cake for church fairs and who never forgot a grandchild's birthday. This spring she had her trees pruned. Lower limbs were lopped off trees near our property line, and around the trunks she planted pachysandra. In September a hurricane struck the state, and one of the trees, which had been pruned and about which she had spent hours digging and planting, blew over, falling along the property line. Compared to me, she was fortunate; I lost a dozen trees.

"You were lucky," I exclaimed when I talked to her the day after the storm. "You only lost one tree," I said, pointing to the one that had been trimmed.

"Whose tree?" she answered aggressively. "The line is not clear." Rather than quarreling and fraying the fabric of neighborhood life, I called a friend with a chain saw. He sawed up the tree. I stacked the branches on a brushpile in the woods behind my house, my neighbor sent over a dish of fudge for the children, and within a few days all traces of the storm were gone.

Picking up things for other people, be they limbs or responsibilities, is hard work. So that one's days will be neat, the temptation is strong to build a fence around lawn and life. Despite the inconvenience of fallen branches, though, I have not built a fence. Neatness does not satisfy; often the chaos of other people's lives attracts me, and I talk about it. Involving no responsibility and even little acquaintance, gossip allows a person to toy with the loose ends of another's life. Endlessly one can spin and weave judgments, bind and unravel without touching an actual fabric. Recently a cousin whom I have not seen for fourteen years has been the subject of family talk. This past spring she went on a Club Mediterranean vacation. For two weeks, she pranced around in the buff and, as someone phrased it, "did only the Lord knows what." At the end of her vacation she returned to Georgia, married a "newborn" pharmacist, and settled down to become a respectable decorator for Penney's.

Keeping loose ends bound is a struggle. Like a rug with a coffee table in the middle and a sofa and chairs scattered near and on the edges, the fabric of one's life is forever being strained. In part I became a teacher because I thought moving from university to university would be easy. Although I have not moved much, I have spent many hours thinking about moving, teaching for a year in white barren deserts, then moving to a land where mountain streams run cold and black. With its mounds of examinations and final papers, semester's end has always been the time to pull out my atlas and dream. Or so it was until this fall. One morning I simply decided that I would spend the rest of my life in Connecticut. That afternoon at Mansfield Supply I bought a crowbar, a pair of heavy-duty gloves, and a gardener's cart. The next day I began digging rocks out of a dell in my side yard. For years I had thought the dell would make a good garden, but I had done nothing because I reckoned I would be moving on. Our house rests on a ledge, and for days I dug and levered up rocks, then carted them away. From the woods I brought up loads of black topsoil. After spreading the soil over the dell I planted bulbs. Not too many, only three hundred or so. I didn't want to overdo the first year; as years passed, I planned to plant more, and my garden would grow magically like a fine Persian rug under the sure hands of a master craftsman. In my mind I saw clumps of sweet William, columbine, and evening primrose blooming in the shade. Beside the rocks that I could not budge bleeding heart and Virginia bluebells thrived. Around the borders of the dell baby's breath tumbled in white clouds while the sweet fragrance of lavender filled the air.

Thoughts of gardening occupied my hours and I was content. Even though winter was in the air, Connecticut seemed lush. No longer did the stump near the property line irritate me, and when I saw my neighbor, I smiled and said things like "Isn't the weather divine." Alas, divinity was short-lived; the skies darkened, and my contentment, like Tom's plans for marriage, was washed away. A week after I finished planting, I received a letter urging me to "consider a move to the University of Florida." Reading the letter nauseated me, and I wanted to cry. For years I hoped some university would ask me to apply for a rich professorship. Now the hope was an actuality, as the salary at Florida was higher and the teaching less rigorous than in Connecticut. But the letter came late. Like a hardy perennial, I now envisioned spreading roots and brightening my small, out-of-the-way dell. "How," I said to a friend, "could a man who planted three hundred bulbs leave without seeing them bloom?" "You have no choice," he replied; "Florida is building a splendid faculty, and you have to apply."

For ten days I did not answer the letter, somehow, I suppose, hoping that neglect would bring forgetfulness. On the eleventh day I applied for the post. "When we move to Florida," I told Vicki, "we can plant all sorts of things that won't grow here. Paperwhites will probably thrive out of doors in Gainesville, and we can put up a trellis and plant jasmine everywhere." For two days I uprooted my garden and, dreaming of oleander and hibiscus, wove a life in Florida. Then I received a letter from a friend who taught there. Writing before my application arrived, he urged me to apply, saying the department had sent out only fifty letters like the one I received. "Please apply," he wrote; "it's a long shot, but you are certainly as good as anyone else and what have you got to lose—only a stamp."

"Vicki," I shouted after I read the letter, "leave the beach umbrella in the attic and cancel the order for the crate of sunscreen, number fifteen."

By afternoon I no longer thought about Florida. Again I smelled lavender on the breeze. Still, I was not so content as I had been. The locust of dissatisfaction had bored up through my topsoil, and I started thinking about weeding and fertilizing. Like Tom, I had had my pleasure, and it was time to pull feathers off something new. If I did not, I decided, life would become as formal as one of Mother's parties. Contentment was for people living highly polished lives, people in whose halls highboys stood like soldiers at attention. For my part, I wanted clutter and dirt: Legos on the floor and crayon marks on the wallpaper. In a life without loose ends, I would be an annual, blooming once and then withering.

For years I accepted platitudes about the importance of writing well. Although illiteracy, I had been told, never excluded one from the pleasures of the bed, it invariably barred one from the delights of the boardroom. The man who did not write well could not, I had been assured, achieve position in corporate America. I accepted such statements uncritically, in part because acceptance was self-serving. After all, if people stopped believing that writing was important, university English departments would be pruned, and I might be lopped off and dumped on a brushpile like my neighbor's tree. In any case, I never really thought about the importance of writing until I received a newsletter from my old secondary school. The school has a good reputation. Its graduates usually attend the best colleges in the country, and the headmaster's job is a plum, providing house, car, country-club membership, and a salary sweeter than that offered by Florida. When I read the headmaster's column, I suddenly realized that good writing contributes little to success.

"Shoddy expectations on the part of a teacher or coach," the headmaster wrote, "have emasculated many a young man and left much potential on the table." The headmaster to the contrary, no gelding has yet occurred in the labs or on the playing fields of my old school. After reading the newsletter, I started paying attention to what educators wrote. I have concluded that as a group university presidents inhabit a world in which linguistic elegance and grace, even precision, are absent. It is a world in which things are forever impacting and people interfacing. Clarity counts for little; indeed, it probably hinders success, making people think one is superficial. Even worse is the writing of the faculty, particularly English professors, the very people who teach writing and who preach the importance of composition. The cutting edge of literary criticism is dull. Dust flies about, and noise reverberating with phrases like "spatialized hypotases" and "critical-methodo-logical catachresis" passes for deep intellectual sawing but produces few useful boards.

The loose ends of the headmaster's prose startled me into thought. By upsetting burnished formality and the accepted, loose ends keep a person alert. Today's disruption leads to tomorrow's activity. The few feathers that Tom took home from years of loving Matty became the sharp quills of humor. Still, a person should consider carefully, particularly as he grows older, before he snatches a loose end. Since composition is buried deeper in the university curriculum than the biggest boulder in my garden, my criticism will lead to nothing worse than a dean's frown. Besides, if things became unpleasant here, I could move to Florida with its bougainvillea and giant yuccas. Loose ends, other than those intellectual, are more threatening, however, than any dean's displeasure. In spring I am talking about composition at a literary conference in Atlanta. Because of my views, the talk has been publicized, and last week I received a letter from a young woman alongside whom the beautiful Matty would seem a swamp sparrow. "Sam," she wrote, "I just learned that you will be speaking in Atlanta in March. How wonderful! Let's have drinks and dinner together." Like the one from Florida, the letter disturbed me. This time, though, I acted decisively. That night I called married friends in Atlanta and bound myself tightly to them for the two days I would be away from home.

Ink Blots

For eight weeks my little boy Francis has been a green policecar. He won't answer to his name, and to lure him to dinner, Vicki and I stand in the kitchen and shriek like sirens. When Francis began nursery school last month, we thought the policecar would be parked in the scrapbook along with the thirty or so pictures I took of him in the hospital and the safety pins that held his first diaper together. We were wrong; nursery school sent Francis into overdrive. In the hall outside the playroom at school is a row of coathooks. Above each hook is a piece of tape with a child's name written on it. There amid the Megans, Patricks, Davids, and Deirdres in big bold print is GREEN POLICECAR.

Francis's behavior arrested the attention of a neighbor. "Identity is important," she told me; "a person should always know who he is. Don't you think," she suggested, "that you should seek professional help for Francis?" The word *professional* frightens me; everything I do is amateurish, and I am going to let Francis race around until he runs out of gas and then becomes something or someone else. Still, the neighbor's remarks were unsettling. When it comes to identity I am not so sure about myself. For twenty years I have lived in New England and would like to consider the Northeast my home. Unfortunately, I have an accent that rolls like the hills of middle Tennessee. Hardly a day passes without someone's asking, "Where are you from?" When I answer "Storrs," people become irritated, thinking I am trying to make them appear ridiculous. If I say "Tennessee," I am uncomfortable because southerners no longer recognize me as one of them.

Not long ago I flew to Birmingham. People like to talk to me on buses and airplanes, and I never have a quiet trip. I suppose I have heard more about "major surgery" than most interns. On this flight the stewardess must have heard me chatting with the man next to me, and just before the plane landed, she came up and as she checked my seatbelt asked, "Have you ever been in our country before?" Not wanting to embarrass her, I answered no. "Well," she said, "the South is wonderful. It's the best part, and you'll enjoy it." She was right; I enjoyed my stay. The only thing that bothered me was that many people behaved like the stewardess and treated me like a tourist from a foreign country.

"Just one of Alabama's peculiarities," I concluded and forgot all about it until I spent Christmas with my parents in Nashville. On New Year's morning the furnace stopped, and when the gas man came to repair it, I went to the basement with him in the hope of learning what to do if it shut down again. I squatted down next to him and, studying the furnace, tried to follow his work. Almost immediately I got lost among the switches and dials, and soon we began to talk, first about the weather, then about the holidays and football, and finally about raising hogs. I felt at ease and, to tell the truth, just a little proud that after fifteen years of college teaching I could still speak the language of plain folks. Or at least I felt that way until the gas man finished working. Then he stood up and said, "I sure have enjoyed talking to you. You know an awful lot about pigs. I didn't know you people raised them in Australia. I thought there were mostly sheep out there." I was startled, and when I didn't answer right away, he asked, "Is this your first trip to the United States?" My first trip, I thought; the basement was a scrapbook, cluttered with things from my past. Leaning against a cabinet crowded with paintbrushes, fruit jars, and buckets of brown, dried wax was a splintered baseball bat. I cracked it in practice in high school, and the coach let me keep it. Behind the furnace was a rusting set of barbells. They were a Christmas present from my grandmother. For two and a half years I had weighed 118 pounds; after eight months with the barbells I weighed 145 and began to play football. From a hole in the foundation above the washing machine, I had once pulled out a big king snake. Stuffing him down my shirt, I ran upstairs and called mother. "Mamma," I cried when she came; "I have a pain in my stomach. Would you feel this?" I added as I unbuttoned my shirt and the snake wriggled loose.

For years my J. C. Higgins bicycle had been propped against the furnace. Although my father had long since given it to the yard man for his son, I could still see it: the sagging balloon tires, the chipped and scraped paint—marks of countless crashes and cut arms and torn trousers—and the squirrel tail hanging from the handlebars. I traded for that tail, giving a new pocket knife to a neighbor who scavenged roadsides, skinning and chopping and salvaging pieces of animals.

"Yes," I answered abruptly, "this is my first trip."

"Well," the gas man said, "I know you will have a good time; people here will make you feel right at home."

"Thank you," I said, as we walked upstairs together.

After the gas man left, I thought about our conversation and wondered if the basement was still part of my life. It seemed to me that someone else had ridden the bicycle, caught the king snake, and played baseball and football. If my past was so removed from the present, what, I wondered, defined me? "You are a teacher," my friend Neil said when I talked to him later; "that string of degrees after your name gives you an identity." If that is true, I thought, I have an odd identity. Eighteen years ago I completed the requirements for my master's degree in English.

Princeton charged fifteen dollars to process the degree. Since I was going to get a Ph.D., I did not pay the fifteen dollars and instead put the money in a party fund. In 1970 I received the Ph.D. and went my way. For some reason this past fall, though, the master's came to mind, and I called Princeton to see if I was still eligible. I was; the price had not gone up; and I sent the university the money. My master's is dated 1985, fifteen years after the Ph.D. This appeals to me and to the woman in charge of degrees. "Most people," she wrote, "argue with me about the dating of the diploma when they are applying so late, so it was a real pleasure to eventually find someone who didn't care." The letter pleased me, and when I received it I took it home, showed it to Vicki, and told her about the degree. Her reaction was different from mine. "Why do such a thing?" she asked. "It makes you look foolish. You work hard and just when people begin to take you seriously, you do something silly like this."

"Well," Neil said, "if degrees don't define you, then your writings do. If anything, you are a writer." People mistake me for many things, but no one aside from Neil, who is a pharmacist, thinks I am a writer. Every weekend Vicki and I take Francis and his little brother Edward to the university farm. I usually wear my favorite clothes: moccasins, torn jeans, a running shirt, and a twenty-two-year-old corduroy coat with no buttons. Last month while I was rooting about at the piggery for some good stones for a boar to roll in his mouth, a nicely dressed man came up and asked directions to the sheep barn. Unlike me, Vicki is a bit of a high-flyer; she wears khaki skirts, madras shirts, and loafers. While I was giving the man directions, she walked over with the children and slipped her arm through mine. The man stopped listening and then, looking a bit puzzled, asked hesitatingly, "Is this your wife?"

"Yes," I answered, "we bring our children here on weekends."

"Then you don't work here," he said, adding, "I am sorry. I thought you did." The man should not have been apologetic; I am more comfortable around animals than I am around writers. A few years ago the Bread Loaf Writers' Conference at Middlebury offered me a scholarship, but I turned it down, saying I wanted to stay home and mow the grass. Although I did have a new lawn mower, and a new baby, and was eager to learn how they both worked, I wasn't entirely honest. I stayed home because I knew I wasn't a writer.

Even now, after publishing a bit more, I find it impossible to think of myself as a writer. Whenever I begin to do so, a reader douses my illusions. Not long ago, after an article of mine on running appeared, an old girlfriend sent me a package. Although I had not heard from her in years, I recognized her handwriting. "Gosh," I thought as I opened the package, "she still carries a torch for me. I wonder what she sent." Whatever it was, I decided, I would not show it to Vicki. At least that is what I thought until I opened the package. Inside was a note and a book. "Saw your article," the note read, "and thought this might be a nice addition to your bookshelf. Best Wishes—Beth." The book was *Stress and Fish*, edited by A. D. Pickering. The chapters focused on subjects such as "The Pituitary-Interrenal Axis as an Indicator of Stress in Fish" and "The Swelling of Erythrocytes in Relation to the Oxygen Affinity of the Blood of the Rainbow Trout, *Salmo gairdneri* Richardson." I did not know what to make of the book, and I examined it carefully, thinking Beth might have hidden an intimate message deep in the text. I could not find anything, and that evening I showed the book to Vicki and asked her what she thought.

"Oh, you poor dear," she said, "Beth thinks about you like you think about all that stuff in the basement in Nashville, fondly and sentimentally but long gone from her life."

"Didn't my article," I said, "stir her and awaken old passion?"

"No," Vicki answered, "it just made her laugh. After all, you are not really a writer."

An energetic and disciplined person might be able to shape an identity. I have tried but have always failed. Periodically I become ambitious and apply for administrative posts in big universities.

Often I make the running and while going through the interviews imagine being "somebody." Then evening comes with the weary return to the motel. As I sit on the edge of the bed, watching television, ambition flows out of me, and I think about moving. I own many prints: Gould birds, Hogarths, David Roberts's sketches of Jerusalem, and pictures of my old Cambridge college, St. Catharine's. When we moved from an apartment into our house, Vicki and I quarreled about the prints. She likes symmetry and order and clean lines, while I prefer imbalance and clutter. For six months our walls were bare; then when Vicki went to the hospital to have Edward I hung half the prints. I hung them in my study and along dark halls, places not seen by the casual visitor. When Vicki came home, she hung the others in the public parts of the house, the living room, dining room, and guest rooms. Invariably the thought of hanging prints in a new house defeats me, and I reject all offers and return home, momentarily content to rake leaves and plant daffodils.

Each year I plant a lot of daffodils, and in the spring when the new grass is up and the flowers are blooming, Neil says my yard reminds him of a graveyard, a long quiet field of green broken by clumps of bright yellow. When I explained that writing did not give me an identity, my yard must have been on Neil's mind, because he responded, perhaps with a touch of irritation, "If nothing in this life defines you, death will. Once in the ground, your identity won't change." Neil may be right, but I am not sure. When Eliza, his first wife, died, my great-grandfather Pickering buried her in the upper right portion of the family plot. Eliza was gentle and kind, and great-grandfather loved her dearly. At his death he asked to be buried next to her. The request did not please Cousin Eta, his second wife, and instead of heeding his wishes, she buried him away from Eliza in the upper left corner of the plot. There was plenty of room in the plot, and to insure that death would not join those whom she wanted asunder, Cousin Eta made relatives promise to bury her between Eliza and great-grandfather.

Once Cousin Eta was in the ground, great-grandfather's identity changed, and what he wanted to be an emblem of his first, young love became a sign of petty jealousy. Like old loves and out-of-date university degrees, death does not define a person but often leads to foolishness and laughter. My grandmother wanted to be buried in Virginia, and when she died in Nashville, the family arranged for her to be flown to Richmond. A local undertaker picked her up at the airport, and by the time my mother and I arrived in Richmond, he had her laid out in a coffin under a huge acrylic painting of Jesus standing open-armed on the edge of a shining gold and purple sea. The woman who had washed and set my grandmother's hair for years in Nashville had insisted upon preparing her for the funeral, and when grandmother left Tennessee, every hair was in place. By the time grandmother arrived in Richmond a few strands had fallen loose, tumbling across her forehead and right cheekbone. Seeing them, mother strode over to the casket and, brushing the hair back, turned to us and said, "It must have been a rough flight." With that she slammed the lid of the coffin, and we left the funeral home.

For someone nearing forty-five like me, thoughts about identity may be beside the point. I know that conclusions I reach about myself will not influence my life. I have no illusions about being the master of my fate; instead I pray just to be able to cope for a few more years with what life gives me. And actually I have not spent much time thinking about who I am. Teaching, writing, getting Francis to dinner, and taking care of the yard fill days and leave little free time. Still, I enjoyed those moments when I thought about my identity and I was the center of my attention. To continue the pleasure they brought I gave myself an ink-blot test. Not the kind of ink blots that psychiatrists use and which look like private parts or butterflies but the sort I found in a box in my great aunt's attic. The box held some two hundred letters written for the most part during the years 1858–78. Most were written to and by girls and boys, then men and women, who lived on farms outside the small towns of middle Tennessee: Columbia, Franklin, White Bluff, and Bellevue. Many of the correspondents had been schoolmates and had attended small boarding schools together, places named Bethany or Minerva College. There were letters to Santa Claus, school commencement exercises, calling cards, invitations to funerals, and accounts of quilting parties, dances, chicken fights, candy pullings, pet lambs, murders, and war. As I looked at the letters, ignoring some while pausing over others, I wondered if my reactions defined me. If I could discover why certain letters appealed to me, perhaps, I thought, I could come close to discovering an identity.

The first letters I looked at were written during the Civil War. I was attracted to them initially, I suppose, by prurient curiosity, the sort of thing that in the fourth grade drew me to pictorial accounts of the Second World War—books filled with pictures of bodies dragging back and forth in the wash of breaking waves. In these letters, though, there was little violence; instead, with wonderful innocence, they celebrated the ordinary. Early in the summer of 1861, Innis Brown wrote Mary, his sister, from Camp Cheatham. "If there is any fighting to be done," he declared, "I want to get at it as I think we can fatigue them very easy if we get afoul of them while the weather is warm." After mentioning the "fine times" he had recently enjoyed with some "ladie visitors from Franklin," he turned to important matters in a postscript. "I forgot to tell you," he said, "to take care of my dogs. If you have not got them, I want you to get them." By December Innis was in Virginia. "On account of sickness," he had been away from his regiment for a month. On recovering, he wrote, he had had "a fine time fox hunting." "There is a fellow that lives about a mile from here that has a pack of dogs and he comes up for us," he recounted, "every time he goes a hunting."

Daily life with dogs and hunting took precedence over war. "There was fighting at Bowling Green yesterday and the day before," a classmate from Minerva wrote to Nannie Brown, my great-grandmother. "My most ardent wish is that the Southrons may be victorious, if the Linkhouners were to gain a battle there I would almost despair, for they would never stop till they were south of me or had driven us from our homes, but God will aid the side of justice, if any justice there be in war."

The war was only part of what was on the girl's mind, and she did not write much about it. She was more interested in love. "Wars nor any thing else," she wrote happily, "can stop this thing of marrying. We had three weddings in one day not long since. I presume," she added gaily, "you are not yet wed, as you believe in sending all *sweethearts* to battle. If it pleases you to answer this, write me a long, long letter, tell me something about your *favorites*."

Accounts of sweethearts and favorites filled the letters, making them green with happiness and hope. "We have had great times, corresponding with Captains Gilbert and Ellis," Sallie wrote from Nashville in 1864.

> The latter wanted me to open a correspondence with a friend of his, Lt. Victor Oliviér. Isn't that name pretty enough to keep a schoolgirl in a perfect fever of excitement for a whole week? I only lost one night's sleep by it, and eat as hearty a breakfast next day, as usual. I declined corresponding with him, . . . though Capt. Ellis says that he is young handsome, accomplished and in short, a gentleman by birth and education. He was wealthy before the war, and belongs to one of the best Creole families in Louisiana. He is related to Genl. Beauregard both by blood and marriage. Still I declined a correspondence with him. Do you think me a simpleton or a prude?

Not all was happy, and on the last page of the letter Sallie wrote, "I expect Aunt Mary will have to take some Yankee boarders in order to get coal. I will not be introduced. We will use the front stairs and they the others, and I will come to the second table. I don't know one, nor do I intend to." Sallie and her correspondents were all about eighteen years old in 1864 and despite the war were able to dream. "Sweet friend," a girl wrote from "Laurel Hill" in November 1864, "t'was a beautifull moonlight night; while seated alone by an open window with a halo of moonshine around me, and the breeze playing with my neglected tresses, and holding in my hand a letter I had just finished reading, that the thought very naturally arose, if Nannie was only here I could tell her of my joys and sorrows." Despite the moonshine and the breezes, life at Laurel Hill was stormy and far from romantic. In the middle of the letter a paragraph stood out darkly in a noonday of realism. "The federals are very troublesome out here now," the girl wrote; "there has been a band of robbers going about through the country. Our house has been robbed twice. The last time they were here they presented a pistol at Pa's head and told him they would blow his brains out if he did not give them what gold and silver he had. They also threatened burning our house and made such wicked threats about me I thought very seriously about leaving the country." Perhaps because dreaming is more difficult for me as I grow older, I was happy, even envious, when the girl ended the letter romantically. She had been to Columbia, she said, visiting a friend who was "full of music." When the friend "would warble in a rich sweet voice, *why do summer roses fade,* it reminded me," Nannie's correspondent wrote, "of the blest days of yore when we were as two souls with but a single thought and two hearts that beat as one."

On November 4, 1864, as General John B. Hood led the Army of Tennessee out of Georgia toward middle Tennessee in a desperate and forlorn attempt to draw Sherman out of Atlanta, Alice W. sent a letter from Nashville to Franklin, to Mary Brown, Nannie's cousin. "Oh! Mary," she exclaimed, "I expect you will soon see some *sweet Rebels,* how I will envy you then, you may expect a visit from me." It is unlikely that Alice had the chance to flirt with many rebels at Franklin. Twenty-six days after her letter, Hood arrived in Franklin with his mind on things other than courting. At three o'clock that afternoon he attacked the Union forces under General John Schofield. When the Battle of Franklin ended at nine that night, six Confederate generals were dead or dying, and more than six thousand men, over a fifth of Hood's soldiers, were casualties. In 1861 Innis Brown wrote Mary that he did not know where the regiment was going. "Some think to Manassa, some to Winchester, but for my part," he said, "I dont care where it goes so they get out of Vaginia." By the time of the Battle of Franklin, most of the Browns were back in Tennessee. Some of the young girls did not approve, and in a letter to Mary, Jennie Brown wrote, "I suppose you have heard that Cousin Joe Brown, has come home and taken the oath, nearly all the first Redgment has come home. Shame on them, Tennessee is disgracing her selfe." *Disgrace* seems too strong to me. When a cause is lost, the sensible man goes home and tends to farming, rakes leaves, or maybe, as in the case of my family, has a drink. If the Browns were not disgraced by taking the oath not to fight again, drink was leading them to misbehave. "Innis," Jennie wrote, "has ruined his fortune, he went to town that cool weather and took too much and went by Old Davis's, and commenct maken love to Miss Dora before the old Folks. He has not been there since," Jennie concluded, "I am going there friday and smooth it all over for him." Jennie must not have been successful because Innis never married.

Most of the men in the letters fared better with their sweethearts than Innis did with Miss Dora. "Oh why were you not at the 'Pic Nic' yesterday," William Bailey asked Mary Brown in May 1865. Although he enjoyed the afternoon, Bailey told Mary that he "would rather live in your company one hour and breath the same air with you, than to live over a dozen such days." Later that month, he cut two lines of poetry from a newspaper and sent it to her, saying, "Please accept this 'Music' from one who, owes to you, the happiest moments of his life, And who loves you dearer, than all else the world contains." "Oh! never woman charmed like thee,/ And never man yet loved like me," the lines read. Bailey's letters were gentle and poetic, and that summer he and Mary were wed. Unfortunately, he lived in her company for just a year. Soon after marriage he was stricken with tuberculosis. Perhaps he caught it at Camp Morton in Indianapolis, Indiana. Some of the Browns and their neighbors from Franklin had been prisoners of war there. "Well as regards the pleasure here at this place," Tom Brown wrote Mary in 1864, "tis useless to speak of, as you have some idea as to what a prison life is, having seen the prison at Nashville."

Bailey fought for his life. Among the letters was the card of "Drs. R. & J. Hunter, of New York, Physicians for the Diseases of the THROAT, LUNGS, and HEART." The doctors wrote long letters to Bailey, telling him how to use an inhaling instrument and advising him on the preparation of embrocations, gargles, and pills. Every week Bailey was to report his progress to Dr. Roscoe at the City Hotel in Nashville or write the Hunters directly in Cincinnati. Among a group of prescriptions was the statement written after Bailey's initial examination. He was twenty-three years old and made his living as a merchant. His right lung was infected, and he had lost weight and suffered from coughs, "Hemorhage," night sweats, and shortness of breath. His liver was torpid, his bowels "costive at times," and his throat and nostrils inflamed. By spring 1866 Bailey knew he was dying, and he wrote his sister urging her to come and see him. "I dont think I have long to live in this world," he wrote, "and it pains me very much to think of leaving Mary. Come—Sister and see us for I will never be able to visit you at home."

That same month he sent twenty dollars to his cousin Molie Cravens in Gainesville, Alabama. "I *do hope*, dear Cousin," she replied, "that you are mistaken with regard to your *health. Cheer up,* if there is any hope in the *world,* and come down and stay with us, and see if a *change* will not help you. If, however, your fears are *reality,*" she continued, "I do trust and pray that you are a *Christian,* and wait only on God's will. Life at best is but a *span* of *vanity* (Save when employed in *God's Service* it is *vanity*) and if we can only be *prepared,* it matters *little* when we *go.*" That summer Bailey died; five years later his wife died of tuberculosis; later that decade Innis caught the disease and died.

Amid the disease and death, as in the war years, life with its courtships and weddings went brightly on. One of the wonders, maybe bounties, of life is that no matter what the folly or sadness, cheerful youth seems undiminished. In 1859 Tom Brown wrote a letter to his "Sweet Little Cousin" Nannie in which he described "EUDORA SOWELL," his "Goddess of love and the Queen of beauty." "She has a beautiful figure, a clear white complexion with two rosey cheeks, red pouting lips, large bright eyes of a deep violet, and a profusion of light brown hair as soft as silk. Her face is oval of that pure *Southern* type which fascinates many a boy and leads him to the *Asylum*. Her mischievous looking head is placed upon a swan-like neck, and inclines towards one of the prettiest shoulders you ever looked at. It is as white as alabaster. Her voice is as soft as the first stirrings of an infants dream, her footsteps as light as the sylvan footed zephyr which first faned with the wing of perfume the gable end of new born paradise." Young Tom did not think he could do justice to Eudora, and after informing Nannie that he had studied himself into a toothache, that Innis had "quit playing the fiddle," and that "a young chap here by the name of Bailey" had written two or three letters to "a Young Lady" and had not received an answer, he returned to his favorite subject, writing, "Nannie, I would that my pen were dipt in the dyes of the rain bow plucked from the wings of an angel, that I might expect to paint to you *the charming girl*."

Eleven years later Charlotte Morton wrote Nannie from White Bluff. Charlotte's letters were as gossipy and teasing as Tom Brown's was romantic. Sadness had yet to touch her, and life lay flirtingly before her, full of promise and intrigue. "Is Hugh Barry better looking than he was last winter?" she wrote.

> Poor fellow, his looks will never carry him through the world. Tell Innis to look his best, I am coming up there soon to see him, if he will not come to see me. I know he will say that I must think I am something great. If Colie gets any better looking I know I will fall in love with him. I have a great many secrets to tell you when I see

you. . . . That evening I left your house, I made a certain young man angry. I had *no* idea how jealous he was. I told him that evening he was over to your house that my heart was buried; but he would not believe me.

At the end of a letter Charlotte asked Nannie, "Please look over all my mistakes as you know I am not a good scholar, and by *no means* show it to *any one.*" Because Nannie was older, Charlotte knew that Nannie's experiences were greater than hers. Sensing that Nannie viewed life differently than she did, she apologized, probably not so much for grammar as for tone. Having done so, she relaxed and concluded with the schoolgirlish request that Nannie keep the letter confidential. In 1860 Mary Brown ended a letter to Nannie similarly, writing, "Please please dont let any one see this *goose* letter." Although youth is always present, those individuals who are young change, and by 1868 Mary was a widow and sounded different. "You ask if I ever feel merry as we used to," she wrote Nannie; "I can truthfully answer I do not. In many respects I feel like a different mortal, have learned that 'life is earnest, life is real.' Amid the changes tis comforting to know the love of true and faithful friends remains unchanged. There does'nt seem to be the same gaiety and life any place there was before the war."

In 1859 Nannie gave the valedictory address at Minerva College. Entitling her speech "Life's Morning Hour," she talked about the future. "In its morning hour," she said, "life is beautiful indeed and glorious as the dawn; but the moments," she warned, "are flying ever. How," she asked, "shall we be ready for the fierce glare of noon and the cool and shaded eve and the gloom of that final night. Above us," she said, "bend the deep, deep skies of June. In robe of green and decked with coronal of pink and white and blue the queen month of Summer makes rich melodies in passing. After her attendant train has passed, however, will be heard the leaden footfalls of the Autumn, tho' hushed for a time as the Indian Summer glides with angel beauty." Life was not only real and earnest, as Mary Brown quoted, but it was often short, and by the later 1860s many of Nannie's friends were certain they heard the heavy approach of Autumn. To be unmarried and forever dependent was dreadful, and those who thought themselves bound to tread the long "*single road of blessedness*" often wrote sad, despondent letters. "The last young lady of my age in the neighborhood," a friend wrote Nannie from Nashville in 1870, "will marry within three or four months. I shall feel like 'one who treads alone.' Those who seem like children to me, are marrying every four weeks. You wish to know something of my future prospects. I have none. I am nothing more than *loose lumber* thrown about unfit for any laudable purpose. My love scrapes are nothing romantic or novel. I visit so little that I have but four gentlemen acquaintances and if one should chance to come along green enough to propose, I feel and know I am not qualified mentally or physically to fill the place of wife." If men did propose to her, she wrote, she would be frightened out of her wits for a few minutes; then, she said, she would "reply in the negative and let them float. I know they lose nothing."

Near the end of "Life's Morning Hour," Nannie addressed her classmates directly. "Let us profit wisely by the acquisitions made here, that we may not disappoint the loved ones who watch our progress fondly. Soon," she said, "the last words will be spoken that we may ever speak together here—let them be words of kindness and love and our memories will be held in dear esteem while blessings will still be asked for us from many true and faithful hearts. This sad hour, too quickly here, will leave from its very tears a rich deposit for affection." For me the letters themselves rapidly became a rich deposit of the past enhancing, as Nannie put it, "the loveliness that borders our pathway in life." I came to like Innis, Tom, Mary, and William, and even poor unschooled Charlotte Morton. For Nannie, though, I felt real affection. Not only could she write but she was my great-grandmother, and I thought I saw something of me in her progress. Until I read the letters I believed I was the first member of my family to teach. For years I had been defensive about teaching, in part because I concluded that I became a teacher only to avoid long hours and hard work. Lately, as many of my old school friends achieved success, either becoming well known or making much money, I grew envious and even resentful. Sitting in my study, writing articles that I hoped would bring a hundred or two hundred dollars, I worried about earning enough money to have the house painted or, more important, to have the dead oak trees in the yard cut down before a winter storm tumbled one across the house. At such times I questioned my occupation, seeing myself not simply as a failure but as a weakling who taught because he wasn't strong enough for the world of business. At least I felt that way until I read the letters carefully and learned that after the war Nannie had started her own school. Among the letters I found a teacher's certificate for the "Tennessee Public Schools." Scoring nine out of a possible ten points on all her examinations, Nannie was certified to teach orthography, reading, writing, mental arithmetic, written arithmetic, grammar, geography, and United States history in the public schools of Williamson County in 1874. Teaching, then, was not something that I had done to avoid real work; it was in the blood, and I decided that I was drawn to it naturally.

"It is an open path that we all are travelling though it closes in the gloom of a forest," Nannie said in her commencement speech; "to all it is more or less agreeable but the forest and the scenes we may there encounter will occasion us to pause. Happy the one who looking forward with hope and inward assurance sees glimpses beyond of green fields opening in the sunlight." By 1870 Nannie rarely wrote about sweethearts; life's morning hour was over, and far along the "*single road*" she seemed to be approaching the gloom of spinsterhood. For some time she had had a serious suitor from Mississippi, but his letters were dull and probably appealed little to the woman who had once urged schoolmates to be active in life and "possess the goodly land and gather into the storehouse of the soul true wealth, before the noons intensity pours forth its wearying fervor." Replying to a letter from him in which he stated that he heard she was going to be married, she wrote in 1874 that she doubted she would ever marry, reminding him that several years earlier she told him that although "I respected and esteemed you we never could marry. I always expect to entertain for you," she added, "feelings of friendship," assuring him that "no one outside of your relations would rejoice more over your settling and success in life than myself."

Nannie was closer to marriage than she revealed or perhaps even thought. For three years she had been courted by D. F. Griffin, known to his friends as Grif and to his family in Calhoun, Georgia, as Bud. Much about Griffin is lost in the past. When I asked my father about him, he said that all he had heard was that "during the war, he had been a sergeant and a martinet." Whatever Griffin was, the course of his love did not run formal as did that of the man from Mississippi. In 1871 someone sent Nannie a letter warning her against him. "A terable hush has taken posesion of my whole nature," Griffin wrote her when he learned about it. "I cant think that you doubt my love and devotion," he declared, "but when I remember that you have some of the most serious and disgraceful charges against me, unless I can vindicate myself most *perfectly,* of these charges and establish myself a man of honor how can you respect me." Griffin suspected a doctor in Calhoun of writing Nannie, but without "positive proof," he said, he could not accuse him. The matter eventually passed; in business in Franklin, Griffin did not have the time to discover who wrote the letter. Truth, however, may have lurked behind the accusations, whatever they were, for Griffin's life in Georgia had not been placid. In July 1872, he visited Calhoun and wrote Nannie. "Have seen every body," he wrote, "believe that I *have* got some friends here, am told so, at least as well as enemies, have seen to the man that shot me, he was working with a thrasher when he saw me, he left his work and has'nt been heard of since, though I sent word to his family that I was too well pleased with Tenn—or anticipated too happy a life to ruin it by shooting him unless he was too conspicuous, but the temptation was almost too *great*—had it not been for *you* I would have shot him six times when I saw him." A strain of aggressive pride ran through Griffin's letters, and he probably told the truth when he said he almost succumbed to the temptation to shoot the man. In 1873 he wrote Nannie asking where he stood in her affections. Instead of pleading his love, he argued it. Always conscious of honor, he wrote, "It is unnecessary and out of place in this to make any protestation or assertion of my declared and known attachment because that could be construed into an entreaty or supplication."

In 1868 Mary Bailey wrote Nannie and laughingly referred to one of Nannie's suitors. "Why did'nt you tell me who your sweetheart is with whom you had the quarrel," she asked; "I think that is a good sign for the course is never straight. If he is not a good, true and noble character I shall not give my consent." By the time Griffin began courting Nannie, Mary Bailey was dead. If she had been alive, I wonder if she would have consented to the marriage. Bud Griffin was not scholarly, and he was difficult and quarrelsome, but I think he was true, and at his death, one of his few friends wrote Nannie, saying, "He was the noblest man I ever saw." Be this as it may, however, when Griffin asked Nannie to marry him, she was no longer young and probably would not have had many more sweethearts. Moreover he loved her and was colorful. In a way he was life's purple equivalent of the rich prose that ran through her writings.

Like their courtship, the course of Nannie and Bud's marriage did not run straight. Griffin seems to have been at odds with people in Franklin. In 1876 Nannie's friends were writing her, assuring her about Bud and saying things like, "I cannot keep my tears back when I think of his troubles. I do not see how they can prove that he is a desperate man." By 1877 Bud had left for Texas to make a new life for Nannie and himself and their little baby, Mamie. He liked Texas, and in writing Nannie, who had remained in Franklin with Mamie until he could earn money enough to support them, said he would do any thing in the world but leave Texas to see you and our baby. . . . Dont let my being among strangers trouble you, because I see a great many men here to like and none to dislike, that is a great advantage that I have here over Franklin and to tell you the truth it was about to get the best of me, my feeling towards some men there. . . . It soured my whole nature, and made me so ill that I did'nt care who I insulted, but I am out of all that now and I hope to heaven I will stay out of it.

Griffin's spirits picked up in Texas, and he enjoyed writing Nannie about "the wildest country I ever saw" and planning a future raising cattle. His letters became tough and healthy. When his jaw got infected he wrote hardily, "I intend to have the whole of the bone taken out if I have to get a carpenter to do it." He was at home in the man's world where adventure seemed just a day's ride off. I understood Griffin's happiness; occasionally I become despondent amid the leaves and, dropping my rake, flop down and dream of places far away from family and little responsibilities, places where a man can really live. Vicki understands my longings, and four years ago for my birthday, she gave me the *National Geographic Atlas*. I keep it in my study and look at it at least twice a week and think about where I want to go but never will: the Sudan, northern Iraq, Mongolia, Kashmir, Oman. My trips with the atlas are therapeutic, and when I close it, I am once again ready for leaves and diapers, toilets and ear infections. Still, deep within me lingers resentment at my family, and though I know it is foolish and wrong-headed, I sometimes blame them for my having become a dull man. In Griffin such resentment was nearer the surface. In answer to a letter in which Nannie had chided him for neglecting Mamie's birthday and in which she had said how much she missed him, he wrote angrily, "It seems to me that I am having too much anxiety from you, intend to try to not have so much hereafter—Yes I know when the babies birthday came, am not so hard as to forget that yet."

While reading the letters, I fell in love with Mary Bailey, Eudora Sowell, and my own great-grandmother, much as I had fallen in love with Vicki. And although I sometimes dream of trekking through the Empty Quarter of Saudi Arabia, I know that for me a world without women and family would be as dry as the desert. Griffin appears to have felt the same way. Despite writing about going farther west, his letters are full of affection for Nannie and their baby. They also contain references to the sexual doings of the local populace, something that Griffin not only thought about but that also drew him to Nannie. "Slept last night in a house and next room to a couple that married yesterday," he wrote, "will tell you something funny when we meet, only a thin partition between us." "Well there is one thing I will say for San Saba," he wrote on another occasion, "there is not a woman in the county of bad caracter that I have heard of and am told by every body that there is not one and there was never but one bastard child born in it and that woman dont live here now. So," he concluded, "you need not be writing to me to be good and behave for you see I have to, but I ought not write this way to you and wont any more, only wish to tell you that, so your heart may be easy."

Nannie's letters to Griffin were filled with longing. "Honey please dont neglect to write to me for you know I cant bear suspense and trouble," she wrote after not hearing from Texas for a fortnight; "to have the blues a week nearly kills poor me. *I do want to see you so bad yes so bad.*" "If you have not gotten into business I want you to come back," she wrote in almost every letter. To lure him home she described Mamie. "There is not a day nor scarcely an hour passes that I do not wish for you to see her. She is so smart and cute," she wrote; "whenever she wants Emma or I to do anything for her she opens her little mouth and holds it up for a kiss." Mamie could say "several words, mammy, dad, daddy, kittie, tow (cow), cat and answers when we call her." Nannie's letters did not bring Griffin home, and eventually she and Mamie went to Texas. One of the Browns probably gave her the money for the trip. Griffin does not seem to have been successful in Texas, or in Tennessee for that matter. Shortly after he left, one of Nannie's acquaintances accused him of leaving Franklin without paying a debt to her father. From Texas, Griffin importuned Nannie to borrow money from her relatives and send it to him so he could purchase cattle. In being improvident, Bud may not have been deeply at fault; the inability to make money seems to have run in the Griffin family. In 1883 Gerald, Bud's brother, wrote Nannie from Cartersville, Georgia, on his business stationery. At that time he was an agent for the Continental Insurance Company of New York; two years later his stationery said he was "Dealer in 'Aultman Taylor' Threshers, Horse Powers, and Engines. And Other First Class Agricultural Implements." In 1887 he had yet another stationery and was agent for the Etiwan Phosphate Company.

Aside from some few letters written during the 1880s, the box of letters contained almost nothing more about Nannie and Bud. Once I had owned a second box of letters, but one evening my father behaved like Innis in the presence of Miss Dora's folks. After taking too much, he found the letters in my closet and, thinking them rubbish, threw them into the garbage. When I was seventeen, I read the letters, but all I can recall now is that Bud and Nannie eventually returned to Franklin. They had two more children, one of whom was my grandmother, and then in 1881 Bud died. I know this because among Nannie's papers was a receipt dated March 9, 1881, and made out from Samuel Henderson to Dr. Enoch Brown. On February 3 Henderson had provided D. F. Griffin's funeral clothes. Bud's suit and shroud cost twenty-seven dollars and fifty cents; his slippers, one dollar and fifty cents; his shirt and collar, two dollars; his undershirt, a dollar and twenty-five cents; and his drawers, a dollar. His socks cost twenty-five cents, as did his cravat. Two collar buttons cost ten cents; his studs, forty cents; and his sleeve buttons, thirty cents. The total was thirty-four dollars and fifty-five cents.

I was glad that Bud died and the letters ended. I didn't really like him, probably because I saw some of him within myself—a kind of Griffin state of mind, self-centered and unsatisfied. I preferred the earlier letters written during life's morning hour when, as Nannie the schoolgirl put it, "the sun cometh forth from the shining chambers of the East" and "life for pleasure ripples as it runs." The ink blots had spread too far and were darkening life close to home. I longed for the Green Policecar to crash into my study and break my mood. Eventually the Policecar appeared, towing his little brother, and I put the letters away, not sure what to make out of them or me. Writing to Mary early in the war, Innis described an evening of sentry duty. "I had a trial of standing guard last wednesday night," he wrote; "but as it happened, I had a good night for the business. There was but one man came to my post, and I halted him, and asked him for the countersign. Then he put his hand in his pocket and drew out a bottle. I touched it slightly and told him to pass on." Maybe there is no identity, and the best a person can do is to touch life slightly and hope it warms his lonely nights.

Foolishness

The preacher was wrong. "Foolishness, foolishness," *Ecclesiastes* ought to read, "all is foolishness." No longer do mirrors bring me pleasure. Instead of wild expectations filled with the music of coins jangling and hands clapping, I dream about the past, silent as a graveyard. Content to walk the narrow, familiar path between home and office, I rarely bark my shins against vanity. Alas, what I stumble over—indeed what has always thrown me, pitched me high in the air and then let me fall heavily and guiltily to the hard ground—is foolishness. With vanity a person can struggle: wear a hair shirt or make anonymous gifts to charity. Against foolishness there is no defense; no girding of the brain can ward off the foolish fit.

Not long ago I bought a birthday present for my father at a mall in Connecticut, not a mall filled with simple shops like Tony's New York Pizza, Caldor's, Mr. Doughnut, and a pet store called "Pet Store." Instead of a jumble of grocery carts, ancient Chevrolets, Broncos with baby shoes or Playboy cards hanging from rear-view mirrors, and new Plymouths with Rusty Jones stickers on windows, the parking lot outside this mall resembled a foreign car dealership. Peugeots, Mercedes, BMWs, and long rows of Volvo station wagons were arranged in neat lines. Inside the mall were fountains, palms in great tubs, restaurants with stars after their names, and boutiques by the handful: Calico Sam's Country Crafts, Green Unicorn Books, Just Desserts, The Cookiewitch Bakery, and Taming of the Shoe, run by Martha and Dan.

My little boy Edward was with me. That morning we drove fifty miles for a doctor's appointment, and since we didn't have to wait for the doctor, I decided to mix medicine and shopping. That was a mistake. Edward is only two years old and under the best circumstances doesn't obey well. When he is tired—as he was when we arrived at the mall—he is remarkably disobedient. In Lord & Taylor I found a sports shirt for Father. It was not easy. Whenever I let Edward's hand go in order to hold up a shirt, he ran away, darting, dodging, twisting under and through racks of clothes. Across the aisle from the cash register in the men's clothing department was a big cardboard box, partially full of trash: wrapping paper, receipts, and empty shirt boxes. When Edward began to pull away at the counter, I picked him up, carried him across the aisle, and stuffed him in the box. Wearing light yellow and green Lily dresses or trousers suited more for the after deck than a mall, the customers at the counter frowned. None of their acquaintance, their looks implied, would ever dump a child in garbage. In truth, with his small hands tightly clutching the sides of the box and his eyes blue and wet with tears, Edward was a sad sight, so sad that I almost took him out when he started to cry. What stopped me was a large woman who turned and said, "How could you?" Before she could go on, I looked at Edward and shouted, "Quiet. If you don't behave, I will be charged with child abuse again."

Although he didn't understand what I said, Edward became quiet. For her part the woman only glared. She started to say something but thought better of it and edged away. In fact, a space opened around me as the other customers moved toward the ends of the counter. I was not wanted, and although I was not next in line, a salesgirl hurried over to help me. Getting rid of me was not so easy, however. Lord & Taylor, I learned, does not accept Mastercharge. My personal check would be accepted, the salesgirl informed me, provided I furnished two dependable pieces of identification. By the time I dug my social security card and driver's license out of my wallet, Edward was yowling and I was weary. When the girl then said she had to have my check approved by the manager, my exasperation broke out. "Good Lord," I said, "a lot of crooks must come to this store. This is certainly no place to bring a child." Then without taking my eyes off the customers, most of whom had moved farther away, I retrieved Edward and, holding him close, said, "Stay near your daddy. There are people here who ought to be in jail."

I felt wonderfully satisfied when I left the mall. What the other customers in Lord & Taylor felt is a different matter, and after my wife, Vicki, listened to my account she said, "Don't you realize the impression you made? That kind of behavior doesn't do you any good. Why," she asked, "do you do such foolish things?" I could not come up with an answer and since then have spent considerable time pondering my actions. Of course I was not going to spank Edward in Lord & Taylor. Actually a few whacks might do him a world of good; unfortunately, I am not the person to do it. I am so soft that before going to bed at night I wander through the house catching flipbugs and earwigs. As soon as I have a handful, I lift a screen and toss them outside. Near me no wasp need fear the flyswatter. Whenever I find one in the kitchen or living room, I trap it in a mason jar and carry it into the yard and turn it loose. Recently a bus I was on broke down near Farmington. We sat beside the road for seventy-two minutes. The air conditioner went out shortly after we stopped, and the driver opened the front door. Beside the door was a hibiscus in full bloom. Hives of bees hovered about it, and occasionally one bumbled through the open door and into the bus. When the first bee wandered in, he caused a commotion, and some passengers favored disposing of him with a quick swat. I rose to the occasion, however, and, catching him and all the other bees that flew inside the bus, returned them safe and pollen-laden to the hibiscus. I am anything but a hard case. Occasionally I vote Democratic. I'm faithful to my wife, never drive faster than fifty-two miles an hour, and throughout the summer keep my yard trimmed and mowed. Twice a week I write my parents and at least once a week telephone them. I was "Most Popular" in my high school senior class and in college was head of student government. Yet Vicki was right. I often make a bad appearance, leaving people with the impression that if I am not brutish I am rash and perhaps slightly mad. In part, blood may be responsible. People in my family are often outspoken. Little inhibited my great-aunt Allie, certainly not the rich formality of oriental rugs, roll-top dishes, and brass footmen. Never a big woman, Aunt Allie shrank as she grew old, and while conversation bustled about her in the parlor, she seemed to collapse deep into her high-backed chair, like a sunken pillow hung with lace and stitched with needlepoint. At least she collapsed until someone said something with which she disagreed. Then from out of the depths of the chair would come a resounding and conversation-stopping "Horseshit."

The pretentious, the prissy, the falsely intellectual, the inordinately sober and formal drive me to foolishness. Although the mall with its curried shops and sleek customers provoked me unexpectedly, I am usually able to judge occasions and avoid people and events that are liable to awaken the Allie curled deep within. Obviously I am not always successful. I have written a fair amount about children's books, and people who do not know me will sometimes invite me to address a group. Not long ago I was asked to introduce a celebrated writer for children to a university audience. Having enjoyed his books, I agreed to do so, little realizing that people came to genuflect and pay homage rather than listen to a man, brighter to be sure and more talented than most, but still a man. I began my introduction conventionally and drowsily enough, recounting my discovery of the author's books when, to be exact, I was twenty-seven years old and attending graduate school. Alas, at this point, I noticed the reverential attitude of the audience. Like a sand castle built along water's edge at low tide, my balanced, judicious introduction suddenly fell away. Reading the author's books at what must have struck the audience as a comparatively late date, I said, was not unusual for Tennesseans. Children in the South, I explained, grew up slower than those in the East. Most of my friends, I recounted, were not weaned until they were twenty. To illustrate my point I told an old country story. Having spent the whole day in the hot sun ploughing, an eighteen-year-old boy built up an almighty thirst. As soon as he put the mule in the barn, he hurried over to his parents' cabin. Seeing his mother rocking and darning on the front porch, he rushed over to her, leaned down, and took a swig. Almost immediately he jumped back and spat the milk out all over the porch. Then turning to his father in disgust, he said, "Damn it to hell, Daddy, Mammy's done been in the wild onions again."

Since my introduction, I have not been invited back to that university. For a time while thinking about foolishness, I thought my behavior was unconsciously motivated by the wish to lessen my acquaintance. The fewer the people who know a person the fewer the demands and the more time one has for one's family. Although this explanation for foolishness seemed plausible, I eventually decided it wasn't right. Foolishness does not narrow acquaintance, but increases it. Although some people are repulsed, many are drawn toward foolishness, and instead of settling back into a comfortable chintz-covered anonymity, the foolish person paradoxically becomes increasingly well known. Although I had not lived in Tennessee for twenty years and had not met the parish minister, I wanted my son Francis to be christened there for my parents' sake. When we arrived at the church, the minister drew me aside. "Sam," he said after we introduced ourselves, "I knew you would not want the new service used in the christening of your son, so I have rummaged through the church and found eleven old prayer books." He was absolutely right; I would rather worship in the lobby of a Hyatt-Regency and read the *Red Cross Water Safety Instructor's Manual* than use the new Episcopal prayer book.

Somehow foolishness was responsible for the minister's knowing my thoughts about the revised prayer book. Never have I been silent about things religious. Not long ago I attended a gathering in which an ecclesiastical dignitary waxed long and pompous about the beneficial effects a year at a seminary would have upon women of the church. "Well," I said when he finally finished, "I don't know about that." From my experience, I declared, it seemed that a seminary "couldn't help a good woman but it sure could ruin a bad one." The difficulty with his idea, I told the preacher, was that it resembled a head with its chicken cut off—brainy but bloodless and apart from life. That, of course, is always the problem with things intellectual and abstract.

Twelve years ago I taught for a year in Jordan. Although I lived a private life, spending my free time writing a book, most of the traffic patrolmen in Amman knew me by the time I left. Occasionally when I went out driving, one would pull alongside, wave and smile, and then tell me about a cousin in America. The police and I were on friendly terms because of some difficulty I had with my car. Amman is built on seven hills, not gently sloping hills but sharp, rocky grades. Laid down in an earlier time when there were more camels than cars, the city's roads are narrow and twisting. Worse yet, there are few lights and no stop signs. Amman is not for the inexperienced driver, certainly not one like me who arrived never having driven a standard shift. Since the University of Jordan is several miles outside town and public transportation is chancy, I needed a car. Because spare parts were unobtainable, cars with automatic transmissions were unavailable. After two weeks of hoofing about, I bought a 1970 Fiat and set about learning how to shift gears. Learning was not easy upon the car or me. Stalled near the top of hills with lines of cars honking wildly behind me, I wept. The car suffered bodily and eventually shed the gearshift rod. Since a replacement was impossible to come by, on the advice of an acquaintance I had the car towed to a garage, the owner of which, I was assured, could "jury-rig a tank." After looking at the gears, the owner said he would have it ready "tomorrow, God-willing." God, it seems, was not a good mechanic; for the next afternoon and the two succeeding afternoons, the car stood dejectedly in the need of repair. With repeated assurances of "tomorrow, God-willing" from the owner, I left Amman and spent three days riding a camel through Wadi Rum. On my return I went to fetch the car. It was not at the garage; unable to repair it, the owner had sent it to another mechanic. Unfortunately, it didn't arrive. Because it had the wrong license plate and wasn't being driven by its owner, the police seized it in transit, and now it was in the police compound, from which, the garage owner said, only God could extract it.

God not having done well by me on the gears, I went to the embassy. Since I was teaching as a Fulbright lecturer, I was their responsibility, and I asked for help. An official agreed to lend me a hand and sent me off to the compound with the Solomon of their local employees. The compound was a large nine- or ten-acre lot on top of one of Amman's hills. Around it was an eight-foot-tall cinderblock wall topped off with barbed wire. Pacing about the wall and standing at the gate were guards carrying tommy guns. Within the compound were 850 cars and a long, whitewashed barrackslike building. Outside the building all was silent as the cars seemed to sink melting in the dust; inside all was chaos. Clerks bustled about with piles of paper and cups of sweet tea. While officials stamped and restamped incomprehensible permits, men gathered in hot clumps in corridors, shouting one moment and embracing the next. It was not a place for the tired or the exasperated, and although Solomon swept me quickly in to see the bureau chief, I was pessimistic and unhappy. After Solomon explained my problem, the chief said there was no real difficulty. All I had to do was drive the car across town, have it inspected, and this included having it driven, and then get a new license. That was fine, I told the chief; the only catch was that the gearshift rod was broken and I couldn't drive the car. Would it be all right if I took the car to a competent mechanic before getting the license? I asked. The answer was no. When I asked if the car could be towed to the inspection station, the chief said it could not, explaining that the inspection included driving the car. If I could not have the car repaired before it was inspected and the car had to be driveable in order to be inspected, what, I asked, was I to do? It was, the chief said, pulling a pile of papers toward him and ending the interview, a problem for God, and that was that.

Despite all his wisdom, Solomon did not know what to do. When he told me that he would think of something by "tomorrow, God-willing," I passed from unhappiness into foolishness. On the way out I asked to look at my car. A guard directed me to it, and I walked over and got inside. The keys were in the ignition. Looking around, I saw that from my car to the gate was a straight eighty-yard run. The boom was up, and the guards were talking and drinking tea. How I got the car into gear I don't know, but suddenly I was roaring toward the gate. A guard jumped up to stop me, but I honked and he leaped aside. Another guard reached for his gun, but I hunkered down invisible beneath the dashboard. Someone else released the boom, but it was too late, and it bounced off the roof of the car as I sped through the gate and turned down the hill. Almost immediately sirens began to wail, and I heard the chug-chug of motorcycles. The police stood little chance of catching me, however. Suckled on television chase scenes, I was streetwise and, spinning through alleys and vacant lots, never saw a policeman. I drove to the embassy. When I got there, I parked, then went inside and told an official that I had my car.

"I am glad," he said, "that Solomon was able to be of service."

"Actually," I began, "he really wasn't very helpful."

At that moment the telephone rang; an hour later, all was settled. The embassy arranged for one of its mechanics to repair my car and even obtained the license for me, sending Solomon with the car to the inspection station. I, the official explained to the police in a mutually agreeable fiction, had only started the motor to see if it still worked. Mysteriously the car jumped into gear, and being a comparatively inexperienced driver, I had not known how to stop it, so I merely drove toward the gate in the forlorn hope that the motor would shut itself off.

Although frustration provokes much of my foolishness, it is not solely responsible. Place of birth also shares the blame. No matter whether brought up in city, country, or town, southern men born into established middle and upper situations of life behave alike. Some cultivate the genteel and try to pass for gentlemen. With outsiders they frequently succeed. Southerners themselves are skeptical, and behind the sideboards burdened with trays and candlesticks and highboys buffed and golden lurk tales of wasted talents, whiskey bottles, and lonely bachelorhoods. Most southern boys don't become gentlemen. At their best they grow into graceful and charming adults, compassionate and thoughtful but not entirely predictable. A vein of the berserker runs through their character like fat through a side of beef. Where the vein comes from is hard to say. Domesticity, the very fabric of society itself, all that world of ceremony that makes civilization possible, is woven out of small, unacknowledged lies. Perhaps manners and charm, courtesy and obedience exact a price that must be paid, and paid, if one is to remain husband and father and part of a community, not in righteous anger but in the social realm's play money: foolishness. Be that as it may, however, the berserker will occasionally out and become the subject of conversation, much to the embarrassment of women and their children but yet often to the affection of male friends.

Many years ago I hurt my hand in a high school football game. To repair the injury required an operation, and since the season had just begun and I was playing on the first team for the only time in my life, I wrapped my hand in thick bandages and played on. By November and the end of the season, the pain had gone, and I was too busy with studies to worry about the hand. Sixteen years later, while I was teaching at Dartmouth, an operation became necessary. My New Hampshire–Vermont Blue Cross/Blue Shield insurance ostensibly paid for the operation, and after a slice here and a pin there, all appeared well. At least all was well until insurance company's computer in Concord rejected my claim. The Dartmouth hospital assured me a mistake had occurred and notified Blue Cross; the company agreed and instructed the hospital to resubmit the claim. Accordingly, Dartmouth resubmitted, and the claim was rejected. Thirteen months, untold telephone calls, and over twenty letters passed. Whenever I, the hospital, or the personnel officer of the university contacted Blue Cross, the company assured us that the claim would be paid immediately. After fourteen months, the hospital gave up and began to dun me, sending letters containing vague references to credit ratings. Finally one morning the head of the university benefits office telephoned and, saying that the traveling secretary of Blue Cross/Blue Shield was coming by his office that afternoon, suggested I talk to him. Although I wore my dark blue funeral suit, blue and red striped regimental tie, cotton button-down shirt, and Wright's arch-preserver shoes, my patience and gentility had long ago unraveled. I began my grievance, conventionally sane. Soon, however, my tie was loose, and I was pacing from desk to chair. When I brushed both hands through my hair, pushing the ends straight up like corn stalks, the secretary winced and drew himself into a tight bundle. When he clamped his heels together, almost as if he were pitching about in a plane during a storm, I knew I was succeeding. "If the bill is not paid within a week, the president of Blue Cross had better beware," I ended with voice billowing and tossing, "because I am buying a pair of pinking shears and am coming down to Concord to chop his balls off. Not only that," I said, getting into the gelding spirit, "I might not stop there. I just might turn the whole damn building into a choir of castrato sopranos." Five days later the hospital called, just to let me know, they said, that Blue Cross had finally settled my claim.

A person never outgrows foolishness. As one ages, though, the nature of his foolishness changes, usually being influenced by his job or the place where he lives. Since I am a bookish person, my foolishness has long had a literary flavor. Twenty years ago when I was a student at Cambridge, a college friend, Ian Southern, invited me to stay with his family in Manchester during Christmas vacation. After our last lectures, we rode the train together to Manchester. A mild, retiring man, Ian had no vices except an addiction to Anglo-Saxon. The day before we left Cambridge the British government had raised taxes on cigarettes and alcohol. At a stop thirty-five minutes from Manchester, four women entered our compartment. They were strangers, and when one turned to Ian and, glaring like the sanctified in the presence of the foul, said aggressively, "I guess you won't drink and smoke so much now," we were startled and silent for a moment. Then literature, specifically Jonathan Swift's "A Modest Proposal," came to our aid. "The government are fools," I said; "they taxed the wrong things."

"What do you mean," the woman asked.

"Population causes most of the world's problems; the government should have taxed babies: fifty pounds for the first, two hundred for the second, four hundred for the third," I added, pushing nicely along once the woman appeared startled.

"What about someone who has had five children?" she asked, obviously being a mother of five.

"Two thousand pounds and compulsory sterilization," I said. The women grew quiet and resentful, and not one to let an advantage slip, particularly since they started the discussion, I forged ahead. Drawing heavily from Swift, I suggested that using taxes as contraception was shortsighted. I had read, I claimed, a report commissioned by the Chinese government in which a high mandarin suggested that suckling children were a potentially rich source of essential vitamins. Not only would the consumption of children solve the population problem but if mothers were paid for their produce, it would be a source of ready cash for the impoverished. Of course, I pointed out, not all women who were potential breeders were married, and since it would be unfair to deny them a source of income readily available to their married sisters, breeding stations could be established. For a token fee, males, I thought, could be persuaded to stand at service.

"Obviously," one of the women said when I finished; "you have never had a girlfriend."

"Certainly not," I answered curling my upper lip in distaste and raising a censorious eyebrow, "homosexual, you know." Suddenly the passing countryside bloomed interesting, and peering intently out the window, our companions did not speak for the remainder of the trip.

In the years since Cambridge, much of my foolishness has been literary. As I write more, however, it depends less on tongue and more on pencil. During summer vacations academics frequently go abroad. While traveling, they invariably mail postcards back to the departments in which they teach. Almost always the cards are arty. Particularly popular are scenes from medieval paintings: long-tailed black devils hotfooting it about in flames while Marys look down cool and serene from on high, or white-bearded saints hunkering down in front of caves in the wilderness while lions prowl the distant desert and buzzards hang in the sky. On the cards professors write "insightful," appreciative notes, bulging with adjectives like *splendid* and *magnificent*. When I began to teach at Dartmouth, I didn't travel much, but during my first summer when cards began pouring in from monasteries in the Alps and chateaux in the Loire, I concluded that if I wanted to be one of the gang I had better go somewhere myself. Accordingly, one bright morning after breakfast I walked to Norwich, Vermont, a mile from Dartmouth on the other side of the Connecticut River. There in a drugstore I bought a card. On the front was a drawing of Vermont; stars shone from leading tourist sights, and in the corners were sketches of the statehouse, a ski lift at Killington, and cows chewing their cuds in a green field. On the card I wrote, "Traveling around seeing the sights. Wish you were here." Then after mailing the card, I ambled back to

New Hampshire. That afternoon the card arrived and although it was placed on the coffee table along with all the other cards, no one ever asked me about my trip. At Dartmouth my colleagues were generally restrained when it came to discussing my travels. During my third year, I made a longer trip, this time to Odessa, Texas. In downtown Odessa is a statue of "The World's Biggest Jackrabbit." Natives are proud of the statue, and it appears on many postcards. I bought one and sent it to a distinguished colleague. "Thought the world's biggest jackass," I wrote, "would like a picture of the world's biggest jackrabbit."

I have three children now, don't travel like I used to, and, as could be expected, no longer teach at Dartmouth. Consequently I don't write many postcards. What I do instead is annotate cards that acquaintances mail back to Connecticut. Last fall a colleague went to London. Interested in drama, he saw several plays and then sent a card on which he listed some of them. Happening to be in the department office when the mail arrived, I was the first to read the card. My colleague concluded his note pleasantly enough, writing, "Am having an absolutely marvelous time." Too pleasant for the likes of us, I thought, and noticing that there was a gap at the end of the card, I changed our correspondent's final period to a comma and added, "so marvelous that this is the first time I have even thought of you sons of bitches."

Actually cards don't appeal to me as much as they once did. As I now think about writing books instead of articles, so cards don't provide enough scope for foolishness and I write letters. Some time ago an acquaintance was made president of a woman's college. Having known him in his purple, less dignified days, I wrote him a cautionary letter. "Remembering your past weakness," I wrote, "I have several suggestions to make concerning the decor of your office"—suggestions that I thought, I said, would contribute to propriety on the part of both him and his visitors. Prominent on his desk in an ornate silver frame, I instructed, should be a large, colored photograph of wife, children and family dog. "Under no circumstances," I warned, "should there be a sofa or a couch in your office. In this sin-cursed world, bouncing on the feathered bed too often pitches one into flames everlasting." On the bookshelf I urged him to put large illustrated copies of *Mother Goose* and *The Wind in the Willows*. On the wall should hang children's drawings. The unfinished nature of such pictures inevitably raises thoughts of the vulnerability of the child and hence the family and would be certain, I explained, "to give pause to any member of the opposite sex who entered your sanctum with feelings bodily stronger than ideas intellectual." About the floor of his closet should be scattered children's toys. "A Raggedy Ann with one eye extracted by tiny hands," I concluded, "would be most effective in deterring those who would lead you into darkness." Unfortunately, becoming president of a college has a way of making weak, ambitious people serious, and I never received an answer to my letter.

I did not really expect a reply. I knew that position is the father of caution. Indeed, like my acquaintance I have been approached about administrative posts in colleges. Unlike him, however, I have been strong enough to reject them. I have been tempted, and once almost accepted a post, but happily, foolishness rescued me and will, I hope, always save me. Foolishness liberates. Serious people of the world, shapers and destroyers, avoid it. So long as I appear foolish, no one will burden me with responsibility. In truth the appearance comes easily. This past February I had an appointment with a dean to discuss salary. The dean was late, and when I walked into his office, Lord & Taylor sprang to mind. Sober-looking people, all dressed better than they should have been, sat stiffly around the room in silence. In Lord & Taylor the customers exuded a smugness nurtured by wealth; here brain, nurtured by education, was in the air, heavy and smothering. Talk, I thought, would freshen things, and I introduced myself and asked people what they did. Unable to slip away to the end of a counter, the room's occupants had to stand the interrogation and provide an answer or two. The air remained weighty until a sociologist told me loftily that her specialization was "the cosmetics industry." Conversation soon tumbled down into the rich dirt as I asked about the ingredients of popular cosmetics. Although she resisted supplying answers, frowning and trying to read a grant proposal, I drew them out of her like a robin pulling a worm from the ground.

What I wanted was something lively enough to blow away seriousness. "Well, if you really must know something odd," she answered in response to one of my questions, "an ingredient of some of the most expensive shampoos, those which provide body, is horse urine, pasteurized, but horse urine nonetheless." "Great God," I exclaimed; "there is an agricultural school at this place, and the fields are full of horses. What are we sitting here for? Let's all go down to Mansfield Supply and buy a truck load of buckets and head for the barns. If we could teach the horses to aim, we could be millionaires in a couple of days." When no one answered—most, alas, resembled that secretary of Blue Cross—I stood up and, turning to the dean's secretary, said, "Mrs. Wiggins, cancel my appointment. Tell the dean I am over at the barns. Better yet tell him to join me; there is enough horse piss around here for both of us." With that I left. This summer I received a modest salary increase, smaller than I deserve and certainly smaller than I would have received if I had sat quietly in that office, mouth shut and hands folded. Still, a modest salary is a small price to pay for not being taken seriously and being left free to wander through days and thoughts without responsibility.

Advice and Dissent

Early this morning I drove to Willimantic and bought two plastic fireman's helmets for my little boys, Francis and Edward. On each helmet is a shield with the number 20 printed on it. Until two days ago, Francis had a helmet with 17 on the front. Then, alas, Edward put it on before breakfast. When Francis came downstairs and saw Edward wearing it, he yelled and snatched it off Edward's head. Edward began to cry. After lecturing Francis on sharing, I gave the helmet back to Edward and he stopped crying. As soon as Edward put the helmet on, though, Francis shrieked, "Mine." I try to be patient, but I have not had a good night's sleep in six months. When I am not spooning out medicine for coughs, sore throats, and earaches, I am going to the kitchen to get juice or changing sheets after an "accident." When the children quarrel over a toy, Vicki takes it away and locks it out of reach in the hall closet. How could I do better, I thought, than follow her example? Unfortunately, as soon as I removed the hat, Edward threw himself on the floor and began banging his head against a bookcase. When I bent over to comfort Edward, Francis tried to grab the helmet, and I snapped. "All right," I stood up and yelled, "if you boys won't listen to me and share, you won't have any toys." And with that I tore the helmet in half.

Little happens in isolation; troubles come in batches. Just then Vicki walked in, and seeing me holding pieces of the helmet, shouted, "What have you done? Don't you know what kind of example you are setting?" Vicki should not have shouted in front of the children; at least that is what friends say, and later when she feels bad about something I will bring the incident up and lecture her. So far I have said nothing because I feel guilty. Vicki doesn't know it, though. During breakfast I was hardily unrepentant and muttered things like "That will show them" and "They better start listening to me." For good measure that afternoon I threw one of Edward's toy cars into the garbage after he refused to remove it from the dining room table. Later while he and Francis were taking naps, I dug it out and, after wiping it off, carried it upstairs and put it beside Edward in his bed.

Actually I will never talk to Vicki about the helmet. Not only do I want to forget losing my temper, but Vicki, if she is at all like her boys, and indeed their father, won't listen. Why should she or the children pay attention when I quit listening to advice long ago? In truth I rarely give advice to anyone except the boys, and then it does not affect their behavior. They are too young to understand much, and once they understand, they are sure to disagree and, ignoring me, do as most people do: learn about life on their own. I say I give the children advice because I want them to avoid my mistakes and be better than I am. That's not true. If the children followed my suggestions, they would become cautious and self-centered, so aware of manners and alert to their own interests that even I would not like them.

Although precautions can be taken against advice, none are effective. Even Big Frank, the Blessings Company driver who delivers diapers on Fridays, dispenses advice. "Have a good one," Frank always says when he hands me the diaper bag. Although I want to answer, "You underrate me; I am going to have a fine dozen," I invariably say, "You bet. Thanks, good buddy." Although some people might not classify Frank's remark as advice, I do. Our society contains so many professional advice-givers that it is impossible for a person not to become an amateur. Advice sells, and psychologists, psychiatrists, teachers, preachers, and counselors and quacks of all persuasions make good livings hawking advice. Above the blackboard in the room in which world history was taught in my high school was a sign stating, "A Word to the Wise is Sufficient." The sign impressed me, and when I was in ninth grade, I copied it onto the cover of a spiral notebook and drew a ring of stars around it. Now I know better; life is complex, and only fools think a word or slogan sufficient for anything.

Although I teach, I have almost stopped giving advice. I have not quit completely, however; like original sin, the urge to advise cannot be eradicated. Recently a student came into my office. Examinations were ten days off, and having been absent since the second week of the semester, the student had not turned in any assignment. When he asked, "What can I do to pass this course?" I succumbed to temptation and advised, "Take it again next year." Still, that was out of character; I don't give much advice; in class I lecture and try to avoid answering questions. I have modeled myself on one of my old teachers. When asked a sticky or untoward question, he invariably picked up a pipe he had put on the table at the beginning of class, reached into his vest and took out a box of matches, turned sideways in his chair, and slowly tamped the tobacco down into the pipe. After lighting the pipe and taking two long puffs, he turned back toward the class and stared at us for what seemed forever. "Gentlemen," he eventually began after we had gotten so uncomfortable that we could only look down at our notebooks, "gentlemen, there are no easy answers." Exactly—there are no easy answers. Unfortunately, few people realize this.

Not long ago at the end of an examination, a student added a personal note. "I pray, Samuel Pickering," she wrote, "that you'll listen very carefully to your born again friends. They've got the answer. This may not be you're idea of a final exam, but I wrote what the spirit moved me to write. I've got life eternal guaranteed, and its wonderful. Do you?" Although the student's grammar was wanting and she did not answer the questions on the examination, I was not sure about life eternal, and in hopes of avoiding advice on the subject, I passed her. Believers of anything are relentless; not even death prevents them from thrusting forward with advice.

Vacations taken with children are never relaxing. Intrigued by new places, children forget the restraints of home, and exploring and climbing, they do things never done before. At vacation's end, only the lucky parent returns home with offspring unstitched and with a voice hale and robust. Last summer Vicki and I took the boys to Nova Scotia. After ten days of warning and lecturing, we tottered in the need of rest. One morning we hired a baby sitter and, leaving the boys at home, packed a picnic of wine, smoked oysters, cold chicken, and apple pie and drove to a secluded cemetery overlooking the Bay of Fundy. While the waves washed soothingly along the shore, we planned to curl up in the grass and doze. Not having had a person buried in it for seventy years, the graveyard was always deserted. Here we thought we would be far from the importuning and lecturing world. We were wrong. After pouring two glasses of wine, pale and bubbly with what I imagined as warm forgetfulness, I set our bottle on a tombstone. Unconsciously I looked at the inscription. The tomb was that of a Captain Amos Hilton, who had died in 1811. "A member of the Gebogue Church," the inscription stated,

> He set a good example to a wicked place.
> You who did not follow his example during
> His life, follow it now after his death.

From the grave came a sermon, and instead of drinking wine until I slipped into careless sleep, I began thinking about the graces which, as another tombstone put it, "are peculiarly ornamental to the Christian Profession." I neglected the wine, and when I remembered and reached for my glass, my hand was too late. Over the glass hung a white-faced hornet, while inside two yellow jackets pushed about and struggled to escape. Carefully I dumped them out on the grass and poured a new glass. The day, though, was tarnished. Thinking about hornets and the stings of life and death, I drank cautiously. I worried about what would happen to Vicki and the boys if I died suddenly and wondered if I had bought enough life insurance.

Although Captain Hilton ruined the picnic, religious advice can be useful. When I went to college, I thought I wanted to play football. A few mornings running in the August sun and a few evenings listening to the coaches changed my mind. "Boys," the head coach said one night, "I'm not blowing smoke up your butts, but your studies won't interfere with your football." In my neighborhood, smoke rose up chimneys and studies were more important than athletics. Quitting the team, though, was difficult. Those who informed the head coach of their intentions were spoken to harshly; consequently, many boys crept away quietly in the night. Nowadays I cut and run whenever any avoidable unpleasantness appears on the horizon; "to stand the course" and tackle something head on seems silly, if not perverse. Years ago, though, I was not so sensible, and I thought leaving the team without informing the coach was cowardly. The trouble was that I did not look forward to talking to the coach. For a time I did not know what to do, but then religion came to my aid. Early in the morning before practice, I walked into the coach's office.

"Coach," I said, "I have decided to quit. This," I added before he could speak, "has not been an easy decision. I prayed about it all last night. I wanted to stay here and play, but the Lord told me to quit, and who am I to disobey the Lord?" Then I turned and started out of the office; at the door I stopped and said, "I hope you have a good season."

"Thank you," the coach mumbled, and that was simply that.

In part my attitude toward advice comes naturally. People in my family rarely listen to each other, much less to outsiders.

While visiting my parents this past Easter, I looked carefully at my father's library. Books were heaped in mounds, strewn three deep behind each other on shelves, and crammed precariously inside cabinets. So many books were in the desk that shutting the drawers was impossible. No part of a table top was visible, and along a wall were piles of magazines and journals. Amid all the volumes, though, there was only one how-to or advice book, *Bad Habits of Good Society* (1883), "A Hand-Book for the Uninitiated and Inexperienced Aspirants to Refined Society's Giddy Heights and Glittering Attainments." Instead of offering serious help "to those parties," as Mentor the author put it, "just hesitating on the plush-padded, gilt-edged threshold of our highest social circles," the book ridiculed advice and lanced social pretension. It was just the sort of thing to appeal to my family, notable for avoiding giddy heights and pitching their tents in cool lowland glades. One Sunday after Aunt Phoebe urged Cousin Will to get a job, calling him a ne'er-do-well and asking him if he didn't want to get ahead, he was reputed to have exclaimed, "A head! I have got one already! Great God, Mother, have you gone blind!" Insofar as anyone can tell, that was the only time in his life Will raised his voice.

"Never," Mentor typically advised, "in speaking confidentially to a young lady of her father's tippling habits, refer to him as an old soaker, a rum-head, a guzzler, a perambulating beer-keg, or a happy-go-lucky old swill tub. Far better," he suggested, "to steer matters gently by recommending an inebriate asylum." The refusal to listen to advice does not imply hesitation to steer matters gently by not giving it. Indeed, somewhere there must be a law which states that the less a person listens to advice the readier he is to offer it. My younger days were filled with advice. Sometimes it was terse—"Keep your trousers zipped." Other times, when, for example, I considered colleges, it took the form of a lecture— "Harvard and the Politburo." Marriage and the birth of my children intensified the advice I received. Rashly I hoped that ignoring my family's wishes regarding Francis's name would be taken as a sign that I could no longer be advised. I was disappointed.

Just after birth, a small operation that I consider unnecessary is often performed on males, and I prevented its being performed on Francis. Three months after Francis was born, we visited my parents. All went smoothly until Father watched me change a diaper. "Something has been neglected here," he stated and after stepping up for a better look, he asked, "Is your pediatrician an American?"

Father then drew upon his experience in the insurance business and offered me a great deal of medical advice, which, of course, I ignored. Occasionally, though, advice is couched in such a way that it is difficult to ignore. Not long ago a graduate student came to my office in tears. Early this fall she had fallen in love, and at Thanksgiving introduced her boyfriend to her family. The boyfriend had dyed part of his hair green, and the introduction failed. Shortly after returning to school, the girl received a letter from her mother. "I come from the Cream of Topeka; your father comes from the Cream of Dayton," the mother wrote; "and I will not accept a PUNK HAIRDO. That's not for this family. He must ship out and you must shape up before you come home again," the mother concluded, "I am not to be put upon. If you don't shape up, don't come home. Writing this letter has been a terrible trial. May God bless you."

"What should I do," the girl sobbed; "I love my family."

"Let me see the letter," I said. Walking over to the window, I read it slowly. When I finished, I rested my right hand on the wall and my left, with the letter on my hip. For a long time, I looked out the window into the distance. Then I turned around; pushing my lips together into a thin line and shaking my head, I walked back to my desk, sat down, and handed the girl the letter. "There are," I said, pausing to take off my glasses and rub my eyes, "there are no easy answers."

If that boy had come home with a daughter of mine, I would have shaved his head before he got through the door. Still, nothing could have persuaded me to advise the student. No good ever comes from making suggestions about love. In fact, much of my reluctance to offer advice on any subject can be traced back to the advice I once gave Skipper, a friend from college. Skipper was clever and attractive and seemed destined for success. The only cloud on his future was his sweetheart, Francine, a girl with the unhappy knack of irritating everyone she met. After college Skipper and I went different ways; fourteen months after graduation, though, we met accidentally in Memphis. In reply to my asking what he had done since school, Skipper said that shortly after graduating he had become engaged to Francine, but he added, "I realized she wasn't the girl for me and broke it off."

"Terrific," I exclaimed but said little more because I was hurrying to the airport. We only had time to exchange addresses, promise to write, and wish each other well. A year and a half passed before I got around to writing Skipper. In the letter I congratulated him on his escape from Francine. "She was a thoroughly unpleasant gal," I wrote; "no one liked her and marriage to her would have ruined you. You are well out of it," I concluded; "take this old boy's advice and marry the right sort, one whose father can keep you in a style to which you are unaccustomed." Skipper and I had been fairly close, and I thought it odd he never replied. Sometime later when I ran into Ira, a mutual acquaintance, I asked about Skipper, explaining that he owed me a letter, adding that I had written him congratulating him on getting rid of Francine.

"There is a good reason for Skipper's not answering you," Ira said.

"What's that?" I asked apprehensively.

"You ought to be able to guess," Ira said; "Skipper didn't get rid of Francine. They got married, and if I have worked the dates out correctly, your letter must have been waiting when they returned from the honeymoon."

Advice can be helpful. When I am undecided about something, I often seek advice. Years ago when I was offered the chance to teach in Jordan, I talked the matter over with friends. All urged me to stay at home; consequently I went and enjoyed a splendid year. One spring Vicki and I found ourselves on Crete with ten more days of vacation then we planned. Because we were not sure where to spend them, I went to the Greek Tourist Board office in Iraklion. Should we travel to the eastern or western part of the island, I asked. "The east, without doubt," an efficient young woman advised me. We, of course, went west and spent a wonderfully inefficient time in Rethimnon. Official advice should always be ignored. Invariably it is tainted by caution, if not deceit.

Whenever I travel, I attend opera. I heard my first opera in Sophia in 1965, a Bulgarian version of *La Traviata*. Ten years later I was in Baku, and having recently seen operas in Leningrad and Moscow, wondered if there was an opera house in the city. The secret policeman assigned to keep track of the group with whom I was traveling assured me that no opera had ever been put on in Baku. He also warned me not to leave the hotel at night without his company. He was so vehement that I knew he was lying. I did some investigating, and that evening after skipping out the back door of a tourist restaurant, I attended the premiere of a Soviet opera sung in Azerbaijanian. The performance was opera as it once was, raw in voice and sincere in emotion. Cries and wild applause greeted the hero's entrances while the audience stood and jeered the villain. Ignoring official advice can bring comfort as well as enjoyment. When I wanted to take the Red Arrow Express overnight from Leningrad to Moscow, a railway official told me there were no first class cars on the train. I listened quietly, then replied that I understood the difficulties of finding accommodation for tourists. "As a token of friendship between America and Russia," I gave the official two packs of Lucky Strikes and asked her to check again. After three visits and six packs of cigarettes I had a private car, complete with servant, for the journey to Moscow.

Occasionally, though, not heeding advice can lead to embarrassment. Fortunately such occasions usually occur during adolescence, that period in which embarrassment seems as natural to one's day as the sun and the moon. Thirty years ago I spent a week at Rock Island, Tennessee, with the family of David, a schoolmate. Rock Island was isolated, and the river provided the only entertainment. David and I spent hours floating downstream in inner tubes, battling in mud flats, and overturning logs and shaking bushes in search of snakes. From a tree perched high above the river, David's older brother had hung a rope. Grabbing hold of the rope, he would take a running start and, swinging far out over the water, would let go and fall into the river with a great splash. David and I were eager to try the swing, but when we attempted to do so, David's brother stopped us, saying we could get hurt unless we wore jockey straps. David and I were only thirteen and didn't own such things, much less know where to buy them in Rock Island. David's brother told us, though, that they were for sale in the drugstore. That afternoon when David's mother drove to town to buy groceries, we rode with her. While she was shopping, we went to the drugstore. Everything went well until the clerk asked us, "What size?" and then added, almost parenthetically, "Obviously small." Not having worn an athletic supporter, I did not know size was determined by girth. I thought something else decided it. If I bought such a jockey strap, my friends, I believed, would think that "something" small and tease me. At thirteen, the thought was not to be borne, and I said, "not small, large."

"Are you sure?" the clerk responded.

"Absolutely," I answered, weighing all of one hundred and eighteen pounds. Would that I had been less certain. I could have wrapped that jockey strap around my waist twice and still had enough left for the makings of a good slingshot.

Today I telephoned Cousin Earl in Fort Worth to wish him happy birthday. Earl had never listened to advice and against family wishes had left Tennessee years ago to lead a mysterious existence in Texas. No one knew how he made a living, but every five years or so, he blew back into Tennessee like a prairie storm, full of grit and tempestuously different. Settled comfortably into rewarding routines, the adults in my family dreaded his arrival and found his presence unpleasantly disturbing. To us children Earl was a hero. As we grew up, looked at our parents, and realized that someday we would likely fall into their lives of finance and insurance, Earl's existence offered possibility and hope. If Earl thrived there was a chance we could hold out against humbug and, resisting family and social pressures, could remain free. Although Earl was now old, he remained my model of the independent man, and I hoped I would be just as unconventional when I reached his age.

"Well, Earl," I said, settling down into my favorite chair in anticipation of an odd recital, "how are you spending your days?"

"Reading writers of a conservative persuasion and listening to preachers on the radio," he answered, "something I should have done earlier. Far be it from me to advise you," he continued, "but . . ."

I didn't let him go on. "Oh, Lord, Earl," I broke in; "I have to go. Francis and Edward have just gotten into a terrific squabble downstairs. They don't know how to share and have been fighting all day over fireman's hats."

"Go separate them," Earl answered, "be firm and then take them to church. They will learn how to share there."

"You bet," I answered and, after wishing him happy birthday, hung up. Of course the boys were not fighting. When I went downstairs, I found them playing peacefully. Each of them wore a helmet, and when I walked into the room, Francis turned to me and said, "Daddy, we know how to share. Aren't you proud?" "Yes, you are good boys," I said and walked away.

Just Started

On a hot August morning, the kind when the heat lies hazy and blue, a countryman sat on his front porch and gazed across his yard toward the road. A neighbor came walking along the road, and, so the story goes, seeing his friend, stopped and said, "What are you doing?"

"Thinking," the man on the porch answered slowly.

"What about?" asked the neighbor.

"Don't know, just started," the man replied.

The story ends here and for me is wonderfully satisfying. If I spent all my time getting started thinking, life would be much easier. My problems begin after I start. Ideas invigorate me, and before I know it, I am off the porch and across the yard. Soon, though, I am entangled in a thicket of thought. Like false analogies, briars snag my arguments while *buts*, *nevertheless*es, and *on the other hand*s cling to my assumptions like cockleburs. Thorny questions block my path and pressing forward to a conclusion is impossible; still, when I turn back toward the porch, green associations wrap around me, and the more I struggle to escape the worse entrapped I become, until finally I collapse exhausted in heap of confusion.

Thoughts that lead nowhere are more tiring than those that go somewhere. This past winter I was so run down from thinking that I quit sitting on the porch until my neighbor Harold suggested putting up a bird feeder. "Birds will distract you," he said; "you will be able to sit for hours without a single thought." For a while Harold was right. As birds darted from sunflower seeds to the thistle and suet, I dozed blissfully free from ideas. I had even begun to put on weight until one day I noticed that in fluttering about, birds resembled the guppies I had raised as a child. Without realizing it, I had gone beyond just starting to think. The bird feeder, I soon decided, was the country dweller's aquarium, while the aquarium was the city dweller's bird feeder. Not only that, but a little thought showed that birds and fish were remarkably alike. When a bird died, it fell down from the sky to the earth. When a fish died, it floated up from the sea to the surface of the water. Within each fish, there was obviously a bird struggling toward the sky. Within each bird, there was a fish longing for the stream. "How bright," I thought and wondered what came next. Suddenly something scratched me; nothing came next and I was hopelessly entangled in briars.

My thoughts often concern animals. When I was small, I had many pets. None lasted long. The Sunshine Bread man flattened Horace, my terrapin, as he dozed in the driveway. In trying to climb out of his box and onto Mother's begonias, William, the chameleon, fell behind the radiator and was cooked. Two boxers ate Mrs. Brown the cat, and during the winter of 1952, the guppies froze when the electricity went off. I buried my pets in the back yard behind the garage and put rocks around the graves. I also clipped the grass over the graves. Father insisted that I do this after he pushed the lawn mower over Horace's grave. The mower threw out a stone, and Father had to have a stitch in his calf. In time the back yard resembled a gravel pit. After Oscar, my dachshund, ate a poisoned chicken and died, pets disappeared from my life. So that I would not grieve over Oscar, Father bought me a chemistry set, and two weeks after I buried Oscar, I dug him up to investigate the reaction. Only a fisherman would have found the results pleasing. Since then I have not owned a pet. I have often wondered why, but each time I start thinking about pets, my thoughts lead me to a world as rocky and as barren as the back yard.

At times I feel bewitched. Even mindless occurrences provoke thought. On the street last fall, I heard a man say, "Far out." Suppose, I started to think, he had said, "Close in." How different would people on the fringe be if their *in* sayings were turned inside *out*. Instead of saying "Right on," suppose they said, "Wrong off." The "with it" people, I thought, would suddenly be "without . . ." Alas, my thought went no further, and no word followed *without*. Usually this would have pleased me. Words cause thoughts. If people around me did not speak, I would have fewer thoughts and be happier. At times I think about not using words myself. Unfortunately that idea doesn't get me very far, and I still use words. At dinner two months ago, when my little boy was playing with his food, my wife, Vicki, told him to "eat up." "Don't be silly," I said; "if he eats up, the food will go to his brain and his skull will explode. Tell him to eat down."

In the beginning, the Bible says, was the word. What appears at the end is left unsaid and, for me at least, is mysterious. In the middle, though, is thought. When the word stops, thought begins and leads to confusion. Not only did "far out" focus my attention on words but it made me think about people who use such expressions. Good manners and formal language are closely related, and people who pay little attention to the one usually pay little attention to the other. Dressed in a worn suede jacket and blue jeans patched with astrological signs, the man I overheard looked like a wilted flower child. What this country needed, I thought, was not urban but urbane renewal. "Manners not mortar" should be the slogan, I decided, as I sat down to write my congressman. Woe is me; I only got so far as "stone walls do not a gentleman make" before the cockleburs became irritating.

Vicki knows that life becomes difficult when I start thinking. For Christmas she gave me a color television and urged me to turn it on and watch athletics whenever I felt a thought approaching. "Nothing," she said, "is more meaningless than sports." For six weeks Vicki seemed right, as I sat comatose and happy through long evenings of football, basketball, and hockey. Then suddenly I began thinking. Sex, I decided one night after watching the New Orleans Saints, was the sublimation of the sports instinct. Normal American boys were born with a hearty appetite for sports and indulged in them promiscuously until they graduated from high school and then found little opportunity to participate in athletics. As a substitute they took up sex. By their thirties few American males played organized athletics, but a great many were married. Sublimation, of course, was finally not satisfying, and this unnatural behavior led to nervous breakdowns, mental illness, divorce, and then jogging, as newly single men tried to get their priorities right. The relationship between sports, sanity, and sex seemed clear to me. Participation in sports, I explained to Vicki when I woke her, reached its peak in males aged ten to seventeen. Few males in this group got married or had nervous breakdowns, although, of course, some boys at the upper end of the group unfortunately imitated their elders and seemed interested in sexual matters. After seventeen, when participation in sports declined, sublimation and marriage began.

Vicki called me a sports maniac and rolled over and went back to sleep. The next morning she said if I didn't clean up my thoughts she would sell the television, and she suggested that I watch religious programs. I followed her advice and, instead of pregame shows, began to watch preachers. One Sunday morning I turned on a block-and-tackle Christian who believed in casting the first clump of dirt. Like a middle linebacker meeting a halfback on the goal line, he lowered his head and let fly at other denominations. The preacher didn't believe in rules and committed personal fouls in every sentence. How, I began to think, could the Great Coach in the Sky let this man on his team? Was there no way, I wondered, to make muscular Christians play by the rules? Suddenly, I thought of the National Religious Athletic Association. If religions struggled against each other on playing fields rather than from pulpits, they would grow rich and genteel from the proceeds of television collections. Advertisers would beat each other over the head with bats in order to purchase time when the Baptist nine with its fifteen million supporters met the Catholic Kings of Swat with their fifty million supporters.

To insure a fair deal for all, the National Council of Churches could become the governing body of the NRAA. Many problems would arise, but these, I thought, could be worked out to the satisfaction of all right-minded people. Divisions like those of the NCAA would have to be established. Of course, there could not be a second or third division, as each denomination believes that it has a unique understanding of the truth. Still, it would not be fair for the Episcopal church with three million members to play in the same league as the Catholic church. Perhaps divisions could be named after angels, and while Catholics played in the Michael Division, Episcopalians could play in the Gabriel Division. On the other hand, the Episcopal church is wealthy and through its booster clubs, formerly called vestries, could offer great incentives to athletes to become members. Split churches would also create problems; games, for example, between conservative and liberal wings of the Lutheran church could not be scheduled, as they would lead to a rash of unsportsmanlike conduct and tarnish the reputation of the NRAA. In certain sports, some faiths would have great advantages. Pentecostals would excel in gymnastics, while those denominations that practice total-immersion baptism would be far superior to all other denominations in swimming. During the first years of the NRAA's existence, in basketball the AME church would always defeat the Congregational church, whose members live in small towns and suburbs. Over the long run, however, establishment of the NRAA would foster greater mixing of races and nationalities than now exists in churches. Few Chinese belong to the Nazarene church, but once table tennis appeared on television, Nazarenes would certainly begin to recruit Chinese in order to become competitive. The benefits to society from the founding of the NRAA would be immense. Reformation of inner cities would take place almost immediately as droves of preachers pounded sidewalks recruiting athletes.

The number of small problems to be worked out would be so large that current administrators of the NCAA could all be given jobs—provided, of course, that they belonged to or were converted by one of the association's denominations. Former officials of the NCAA would certainly be adept at dealing with religious teams that already exist, those, for example, at Wake Forest and Notre Dame. Some changes in halftime entertainment would be necessary. Mascots would be forbidden; few teams would play Snake Handlers if they brought tubfuls of their pets along. Cheerleaders might disappear, particularly in games played by the Amish or Mennonites. Much attention would have to be paid to injuries to prevent faith healers from sending players with broken legs and arms back on the field. Minor adjustments would have to be made in scheduling. While fundamentalists, as I explained to Vicki, would always want to play hardball, latitudinarians would insist upon softball.

"Think how exciting games would be," I said to my neighbor Harold, "players who were born again or believed in deathbed repentance would never give up."

"All well and good," Harold answered; "but since you don't have a television anymore, you should give up the idea. Vicki was right. You have thought enough. What you need is a trip."

"Oh, Lord," I started to think, "not my last train trip."

I lived in Vermont at the time. I was invited to Washington and decided to ride Amtrak. At 12:30 at night I boarded the train at White River Junction and, finding an empty seat, fell asleep. Toward morning I dreamed I was caught in a thunderstorm and woke up. A seven-year-old boy was spitting in my face. Just as I reached out to cut off his spigot, a large woman in gray dress said, "Johnny, stop that and come here. I hope," she added, "he hasn't bothered you."

"No," I said as I reached for my handkerchief. "Oh, well," I thought as I wiped my forehead and looked at my watch, "things could be worse." It was seven-thirty and we would soon be in New York. Suddenly I realized the train was not moving. I looked out the window and saw the sun rise over the Absorbine Jr. factory in Springfield, Massachusetts. The engine had broken down and we were on a siding. Those things which could have been worse got worse. The heat went off, and I unpacked my suitcase and put on a sweater and another pair of socks. At 2:30, after seven cold hours, the train finally reached New York. On arrival, an official told me Amtrak had been cancelled and directed me to the regularly scheduled New York–Washington train. Unknowingly I had gone from the icehouse to the nuthouse.

I sat down across from a pleasant man with a cigar box in his lap. After I settled in, he leaned over and asked, "Would you like some refreshment?" Then he opened the box; pills of all sizes and colors were crammed inside. After I refused, he said, "I hope you don't mind if I have some. They make the trip easier." With that he swallowed a handful and shut his eyes. Too polite to change my seat and apprehensive that he might do something irrational if he found me staring at him, I watched people entering the car. In the aisle ahead a small man struggled to push a cardboard suitcase onto the rack above a woman wearing green pants and a pink blouse. The man stood on his toes, and when the train suddenly lurched, he dropped the suitcase, and it fell on the woman's head. She jumped out of her seat and, looking around angrily, strode down the aisle and grabbed me. "You saw it," she yelled; "should I sue him for brain damage?" If my traveling companion had opened his cigar box just then, I would have been thankful. Unfortunately he was in another world, and all I did was say, "No ma'am, the suitcase was cardboard and you'll be fine."

"You think so," she said; "feel this." And with that she grabbed my hand and pressed it on her head. My trip was not for the fastidious; there was enough grease on her hair to baste a twenty-pound Christmas turkey. I slipped my hand across her head and reassured her that she was all right. "No thanks to that jackass," she said, pointing at the little man whose suitcase had fallen on her. "Get off this car," she shouted. The little man moved quickly; before the train was out of the station, he and his suitcase had disappeared.

For a while all was peaceful. I noticed, though, that a man across the aisle repeatedly went to the lavatory. Each time he got up, his wife tried to stop him. "What a dreadful woman," I thought, "torturing a poor man with a bladder problem." Still, the man's difficulties were not my concern, and I started to fall asleep. Suddenly someone shook me and yelled in my ear, "Is this Jacksonville? You," I heard, "is this Jacksonville?" The man with the bladder problem had left the car, not for medicine but for a more powerful tonic.

"Not yet," I answered, hoping he would be satisfied; "we are not in Jacksonville yet."

For ten minutes he was quiet; then he turned and, looking at me, yelled, "Is this Jacksonville?" All hope of sleep vanished, and until we stopped at a commuter station on the outskirts of Washington, I was an authority on Jacksonville. When the train stopped in the station, the man glared at me and, after shouting, "You don't know anything," got off the train. As we left the station, his wife shrieked and rushed down the aisle toward me. Pushing me over, she sat down and cried, "We were going to Jacksonville." She had sampled her husband's tonic, and her sobs woke the man with the cigar box. Gazing at her benevolently, he said, "I feel sorry for you. But worse things happen. Last month I was stabbed. Let me show you the scar." When he started pulling out his shirttail, I headed for the lavatory in the forlorn hope that the traveler to Jacksonville had forgotten his bottle.

Like an idea, the trip had started easily. But the events, resembling examples in a poor inductive argument, jumbled chaotically together and left me worn out and almost as confused as if I had been thinking. I could not decide what to think about the trip. All I knew was that I did not want to take another one. "No, no," I said to Harold, "I can't take a trip." "Well, then," he said, looking out the window, "let's go to the beach. It is a beautiful day. The rest will do you good, and tomorrow you will feel like a new man." Harold was right; on the beach people bake instead of think. Occasionally soccer players kick sand about, but little happens to provoke thought. Even the colors are dull: the sky and water are blue; the sand, white; and the bodies, brown—or so they used to be.

Even before I rubbed on suntan lotion I noticed the tattoos. Although roses and daisies grew on shoulders and hips, honeybees buzzed around navels. Hearts and "mother" appeared on arms while eagles nested on chests and snakes curled about ankles. People who were never noticed, I thought, got tattoos to call attention to themselves. If they really wanted to stand out, instead of having a mermaid or a lion tattooed on them, they should, I thought, have their pictures tattooed on lions or mermaids. "Harold, imagine," I exclaimed, "what a sensation there would be if a man showed up at a tattoo parlor with a lion or mermaid on a leash. Better yet," I continued, "suppose he brought his mother on a rope and demanded that his picture be tattooed on her back."

"Far out," Harold answered. Then I said . . . but, of course, you know what I said. Harold then said I gave him a headache and asked me if I had any aspirin. That reminded me of my trip on Amtrak. After I described it to him, Harold became angry and told me to shut up. I told him that he should have said "shut down," explaining that machines became silent when they were shut down. Harold glared at me and then said I was for the birds.

That reminded me of the relationship between birds and fishes. By the time I had finished describing the pets I had owned, Harold had left.

I telephoned Vicki and she came for me. She asked what upset Harold. I told her, and she said he wasn't a good sport. "Ah," I said, "that's it," and explained that Harold's sex and sports lives had obviously been confused since adolescence. "Jesus," Vicki said. That reminded me of the NRAA, and if Vicki had not been an urbane woman of the world, I would still be at the beach. Instead, here I am on the front porch. I am not doing anything, but I see someone coming along the road.

Pictures

I liked the picture on our Christmas card this year. Vicki took it one October morning after I had been raking leaves. She brought a kitchen table into the yard, and while Francis, Edward, and I sat in a big pile of leaves, she put the camera on the table and, after setting it on automatic, ran over and dropped down beside us. "How did you like the card," I said while visiting my parents in Nashville during the holidays. "Well," Mother answered, "at least you can't see the garbage cans." Last year Vicki took the picture in the side yard near the garage. Although she didn't notice them at the time, our garbage cans were in the background. When the picture came back from the developer, Vicki saw the cans and asked me if we should use it on the card. I said yes, arguing that the cans were "us." Instead of being plastic tubs that hardly made a sound when trundled out to the road, they were metal and behaved like real garbage cans. Whenever a wind overturned them, their tops blew into neighbors' yards and their bottoms clattered down the driveway and crashed into the woodpile. I usually heard them tumbling about and, feeling comfortable, invariably said, "Listen to that wind; there's going to be a storm."

My idea that the cans somehow revealed a real us did not impress Mother. "If it is honesty you are looking for," she said, "take the next picture in the bathtub." Mother had a point, and this year we made sure that there were no cans in the background. Of course putting a family picture on a Christmas card is hokey. Not many people we know do it. The literary folk among our acquaintance send cards depicting nativity scenes taken from medieval psalters, while businessmen and doctors send cards with illustrations of spare Scandinavian Christmas trees or Santa Claus hurrying about in a Mercedes loaded with smoked salmon and Johnnie Walker. Still, I thought Mother would like this year's card, and when she did not, I examined all the cards she received. She kept them in a silver, shell-shaped nut dish in the living room. Our card wasn't among them, and it wasn't there, I decided, because it was too informal for the room. In the few cards with family photographs, people wore their best clothes. Mothers and fathers dressed in grays and dark blues with touches of red and green here and there. Little girls wore pink dresses and white leather shoes, while little boys wore short pants suits and shirts with Peter Pan collars. Deep in the leaves the overalls our boys wore were not noticeable, and Vicki, wearing an orange and yellow sweater, looked like autumn itself. The trouble with the card was me. I wore a blue and white T-shirt. On the front was a profile of an Indian with three feathers in his hair; above his head was printed "Tarzan Brown Mystic River Run."

What a good race it had been, I recalled as I thought about the card, a sunny day along a road near the tall ships at Mystic, and I had run well. For my parents the shirt evoked no memories, and, seeing only unseasonable and indecorous dress, they longed for the formality traditionally associated with holidays. That formality, however, is often as posed as holiday snapshots. Life is frayed around the collar, wears T-shirts, and rakes leaves. By bringing things into ordered perspective, photographs distort living. Not long ago Vicki and I received a packet of pictures from a relative with whom we spent Thanksgiving. The scenes in the pictures were arranged. On the dining room table were a linen tablecloth and napkins, ornate nineteenth-century candelabra, silver goblets, and plates with blue and gold bands running around the edges. Wild rice, turkey, beans with mushrooms, sweet potatoes, and a score of cut-glass dishes containing brightly colored condiments rested on the sideboard. Beside it stood our hostess, knife and fork in hand, ready to serve the meal. The people sitting around the table were smiling and seemed happy and relaxed. The smiles, however, were just clothes put on for the occasion; beneath them was tension. Our hostess was an alcoholic; barely able to stand for the picture, she collapsed and had to be carried to bed halfway through the meal. Most people had left when she reappeared four hours later, explaining, "That was the worst sinus attack I have ever had."

As clear photographs blur truth, so correspondingly, and perhaps fittingly, an individual's perspective distorts clarity. When looked at through the long lens of living, no event is ever what it first seems. In one of the simplest photographs we received, our little boys and their cousins sat on a couch. In his hand each child held a toy pilgrim or turkey. The photograph was balanced; the five children were evenly spaced out; on each side of the couch was an end table; on top of each was an arrangement of yellow and white chrysanthemums. On the back of the photograph, our hostess drew a smiling face and wrote, "HOW CUTE!!!" Cute the children may have been, but when I first looked at the photograph I did not see them. Instead I noticed a small green and gold china pelican on one of the tables. It was Herend china; for some time I had given Herend figurines to close relatives for Christmas. "It was funny how that began," I thought as I held the picture. Years ago in London I had gone to Asprey to buy a leather satchel to hang over my shoulder. Many men in London wore them, and I thought one would make a good carrying case. Asprey is an expensive store; a footman in top hat and tails opens the door for customers, and the saleswomen look like rich aunts from the right part of the country. I was ill at ease, and when a woman asked if she could help me, I found it difficult to describe what I wanted.

"I'm looking for a pocketbook to throw over my shoulder," I said. When the woman did not respond immediately, I hurried forward, adding, "You know, the kind homosexuals carry."

"They are not," the woman answered after a pause, "all homosexual. Some are French."

"Oh," I said, feeling and probably sounding like a punctured balloon, "I guess I don't want one." Then glancing quickly around in hopes of finding something else to talk about so I would seem less foolish, I asked, "I need to buy my mother a present. Do you have any suggestions?"

"Ah," the woman answered, "we have just received a shipment of Herend china; the figurines make most attractive gifts."

After putting my parents' Christmas cards back on the dish, I stood up and, glancing around, noticed that there were no photographs in the room. On the walls were paintings and portraits and an occasional print; photographs were in the back, private part of the house, on chests and night tables in bedrooms and on shelves in dressing rooms. Unlike the portraits, which seemed permanent and had hung in the same places as far back as I could remember, photographs appeared ephemeral. Whenever Mother received new pictures of Edward and Francis, she forced them into frames in front of old pictures. When the frames became filled and started to bow, she took the old pictures out and stuffed them carelessly into a box at the top of her closet. Throughout the house were boxes like this, out of sight and cluttered with photographs and remnants of time past.

In my old bedroom was a sugar chest filled with scrapbooks. The first part of each scrapbook was organized with pictures and papers arranged neatly. Like life, though, the scrapbooks soon got out of hand, and at the end of each book pictures were pushed in haphazardly; the bindings of the books split, and, like stones eroded from the face of a cliff by wind and water, negatives had slipped loose and rolled through layers of memories to litter the bottom of the chest. My scrapbooks were on top, and I wanted to hurry through them. Pictures of myself usually make me uneasy. When Vicki brings a group back from the developer, I look at them once, then consign them to the attic. Returning to them months and even years later embarrasses me and makes me feel guilty. As I age and my world constricts, I do not want to confront my past and be compelled to judge it and then regret life missed. This time, however, I went slowly through the scrapbooks and looked at each picture. I am not really sure why. Because I had examined the photographs on my parents' Christmas cards almost dispassionately, maybe I started out interested in the photographs simply as photographs. Whatever my motivation, however, I soon left the world of the abstract and entered that of the personal.

In scrapbooks, pictures are not isolated; letters, newspapers, cards, written materials of all kinds frame them. In one book, I found a letter addressed to "3rd Lt. Sammy." Mailed to me from El Paso in October 1945, it was from Jack Spore, who lived with his relatives in an apartment on the same landing as ours. Jack was about to be discharged from the army, and he wrote, "Tell Tigue and Kaka I may be home sooner than they expect—and to have plenty of coffee on hand so you and I can drink our coffee together." I have always been a poor athlete, but in school, I tried hard and played just about everything, in the process suffering untold anxiety. As I read Jack's letter and looked at pictures of me holding football helmets, tennis rackets, and baseball bats, I remembered a football game my junior year in high school. The game was important, and since I was a rarely used substitute, I did not expect to play. At the end of the third quarter, we led by two points, but the other team made a first down on our eight-yard line and appeared certain to score. The evening was cool, and despite the excitement I was dreaming blissfully and safely in the middle of the bench when I heard, "Pickering, get in there at left tackle." The coach had made a mistake, and when the other team came out of its huddle, I prayed they would run the ball the other way. Just before the ball was snapped, though, the referee blew his whistle and approached me. It was Jack Spore. I had not seen him for eight years; at the end of the third grade, my parents and I moved into a house in the suburbs. "Sammy," Jack said loudly, "if you hurt any of these boys, I am going to tell your Mommy and Daddy." Then blowing his whistle again, he shouted, "Play ball."

Although scrapbooks are filled with tokens of success, looking through one brings failure sharply to mind. "He has achieved what I predicted for him when he came here," a dean of my college wrote to my parents twenty-five years ago, "he's our finest type, and we are grooming him for a Rhodes Scholar Candidate—I hope you'll encourage him in this." My parents followed the dean's suggestion, but as this year's Christmas card illustrated, grooming has never done much for me. On the same page as the letter was a photograph of a friend and me going rabbit hunting in 1960. I still have the jacket I wore in the picture. Although it has more tears than buttons, I wear it everywhere in the fall. "Did you make that coat?" a university administrator asked me when I walked into his office. "No," I answered. "Well, you sure fooled me," he said, "because it looks like you made it— in the garage with a hammer and nails."

I fell in love for the first time in nursery school, but love didn't become a nuisance until the sixth grade. That year Santa Claus brought me a book entitled *for BOYS only*. In it a Dr. Richardson lectured schoolboys on proper behavior with girls. "There are lots of ways of having good times with girls. Let's not choose the wrong ones," he urged. In the sixth grade following the good doctor's advice was easy. Sadly, that happy state of simplicity lasted only a few years. In the scrapbooks were pictures of Irene, Alice, Becky, Pam, Rita, and a classroom of others. Times always seemed to start out "good," but inevitably they ended wrong;

smiles turned into frowns, and bright interest became boredom. Among my old loves was a picture of Vicki. Her hair hung over her shoulders, and she wore jeans, a green cashmere sweater, and a double string of pearls. Her right hand rested jauntily on her hip, her eyes were laughing, and her mind was on love. Now Vicki's hair is short like a boy's. She wears support hose to shore up veins broken down by three quick pregnancies, and when she travels, it is not with love on her mind but earaches, antibiotics, and cough syrup.

People sentimentalize while looking through scrapbooks and often imagine meeting old loves and friends. Characters in photographs are not real and can be controlled, buried deep for years then dug up and molded to suit a whim. Actual people do not behave so conveniently, and if faced with the choice of renewing a long-interrupted friendship or looking at a picture and creating a past and a future, I suspect most people would choose the photograph. As a boy I spent summers on my grandfather's dairy farm in Virginia; during those years my closest friends were the Cutter boys, five country children with whom I lived days of building, catching, and exploring. In the scrapbooks were several photographs of us together. Looking at the boys, I wondered where they were and imagined our meeting. What a lot we had to talk about. Would they remember the sliding hill, the bamboo woods, and the mud turtles we fished out of a swamp near the Tappahanock and turned loose in the spring? Would they know what finally happened to the crazy man who broke into the dairy, telephoned the house, and threatened to cut my throat? For two days he roamed through the woods eluding the sheriff and a posse of searchers. Even as I drifted along in the comfortable shade of memory, I knew I was only indulging myself. My life had diverged sharply from those of the Cutters, and I had become part of a safe formality. Although my clothes are tattered and formless, at the core I am acutely sensitive to propriety and knew I did not want to entertain the Cutters. Two of them had been in prison, and I realized little good would come from our meeting.

Two years ago James Cutter called Mother in Nashville and asked for my address, saying he wanted to visit me. Mother told him I was out of the country and would not be back for at least four years. When Mother told me what she had done, I wanted to cry, "oh, Mother, how could you? We were best friends." Instead I said, "Thank you, you did the right thing."

Outside Nashville on the road to Chattanooga, there used to be a modest white clapboard church. In front of the church was a sign reading "Founded on Calvary in 33 A.D." Nashville has grown, and the Chattanooga highway has become an interstate, too busy and expensive for little churches and bordered instead by shopping centers, condominiums, motels, and restaurants. Like my memory of the Chattanooga road, scrapbooks always contain pictures of places long gone. With stalls for horses and cars, the garage of Grandfather Ratcliffe's house outside Richmond was larger than the house in which I now live. After the house burned, Grandfather bought Cabin Hill, a farm deep in Hanover County. Redoing the house was a labor of love, and near its completion, when I was four and a half, Grandfather wrote me. "This beautiful picture on the back of your letter," he said, "I will hang up in my new house that I am having fixed, and I do not want any little boys to pull any of the paper off of the wall, and if they do, it is no telling what will happen to them. I am fixing everything as nice as I know how," he continued; "I am working my finger nails to the bone to get food for you and your Mother when you get here." With magnolias throughout the grounds, long rows of pink and white dogwood along the drive, and a forest of boxwood about the house, Cabin Hill bloomed like spring in an album of pictures. The reality now resembles autumn. The farm has been divided, and the gardens ploughed under for a housing development. Even worse was the fate of Grandfather Pickering's home in Carthage, Tennessee. In one picture my father and his brother Coleman, aged six and four, stood in front of a two-story Victorian house. A porch wrapped around two sides of the house; on it were a swing, rocking chairs, and a child's hobbyhorse. Behind the house long gray fields sloped down toward the Cumberland River. The house doesn't exist now; four years ago it was torn down to make room for a Ben Franklin variety store. Since my memories of Cabin Hill and Carthage are clear, the photographs frightened me. Instead of eliciting sweet reveries, they made me aware of the evanescence of things and my mortality, built not upon stone and wood but upon soft flesh and brittle bone.

In the sugar chest were many items from my parents' pasts. Two of my father's baby teeth were in an envelope labeled "Samuel's First Teeth Shed, June 1915, Age 6 Years, 11 Months." In another envelope supplied by "The City Barber Shop. Sam King, Proprietor. North Side Public Square. Carthage, Tennessee Box 201" was a lock of Father's hair. The color was a kind of fawn blond, just the same as Edward's, and I showed it to Vicki and Mother and Father. Although the childhood mementos of people whose lives were quickly gathering toward an end are endowed with pathos, finding the envelopes pleased me. The similarity between Father's and Edward's hair linked generations and seemed a sign of continuation. Although I looked at the mementos of my parents' childhoods, I hurried through the photographs and keepsakes of their adolescence and young, unmarried years. In a jewelry case in the attic, I found the love letters Father wrote Mother before they were married. When I saw the handwriting and read the postmark on the first envelope, I knew what the letters were, and I quickly closed the jewelry box. My children and their children could read them, not I. The only photographs I paused over that showed my parents as young adults were those in which I appeared. After my birth, their worlds were mine. Before I was born, their lives seemed private. Mother was lovely, and when I found pictures of her at dances at Princeton and Washington and Lee, showing dalmatians at the Orange Lawn Tennis Club, and shooting trap on Long Island, I felt like a voyeur. Pictures of distant relatives did not affect me the same way. A photograph of a great-grandmother with lace billowing up to a buttonlike gold earring in one ear and then rolling in rich curves over her shoulders reminded me of Annie, an old love rounded and warm as the damp summer earth.

Not all the pictures of Mother as a young woman bothered me. Occasionally something on the edge of a photograph caught my attention. On the way to the Maryland Cup Race, Mother, her date, and another couple stopped for a picnic. In the background of the picture was their car, a wonderfully boxy Rolls-Royce, a car I now associate with the pampered rich but one in which I would like to travel once. I want to feel special. A single ride, though, would be enough; more might corrupt me and make me think I was superior. Mother's date for the race was Ernest. Although Ernest had been her best beau for a time, I did not mind looking at him. His expression was bland and had none of the seductive power of the bold, appraising glance that marked photographs of Father in the 1930s. Ernest was certain to be disappointed in love, and I traced his courtship up to the telegram he sent on the eve of Mother's wedding, apologizing for not attending. "TERRIBLY DISAPPOINTED," it read; "BUSINESS ENGAGEMENTS PREVENT BEING THERE STOP MY SINCEREST BEST WISHES ERNEST."

In the library were several family albums. Bound in leather, they resembled books from the back; across the front ornate metal buckles clasped them shut. Inside were pictures taken from the 1860s through the 1880s. Unlike the people in the scrapbooks, few of these people were immediately identifiable. There were women with heavy stovepipe curls, in dark dresses bound at the neck by brooches, or with roses in their hair; little girls in high-topped button boots and bloomers; boys wearing new hats and checkered vests out of which hung watch chains; and soldiers—three young men in Confederate uniforms, then a Union captain with his hair slicked down, who signed his picture "Yours Truly Tom Waters." Exchanging pictures was fashionable in the last part of the nineteenth century, and every town had a photographic studio. On the back of a picture was the photographer's name and address: B. W. Rose, Corner, Main &

Broadway, Paris, Kentucky; J. H. Van Stavoren's Metropolitan Gallery, 53 College Street, Nashville, Tennessee; A. D. Lytle, Main Street, Baton Rouge, Louisiana. My great-grandfather came from Ohio, and the albums contained photographs taken in Athens, Cincinnati, Portsmouth, and Springfield. Unlike this year's Christmas card, which turned my thoughts inward to Mystic and memory, the photographs thrust me outward as I tried to identify people in the pictures.

I started leafing through old books in the library. The going was slow, and soon what I searched for was less important than what I found. In a family Bible was a copy of the *Athens Messenger* for January 12, 1899. My great-great-grandfather's obituary was on the front page. "During the last week," the article recounted, "he grew gradually more infirm, and early Sunday morning, after he had journeyed long and journeyed far, there came for him the twilight and the dusk, the mist gathered over the mirror of memory, the pulse throbbed faint and low, and finally ceased to beat on earth forever." Like catacombs into which individuals disappear to become part of great heaps of bones, the yellow, spotted pages of the Bibles reeked of death and families gone from memory. Unlike the death that stalks through my days, making me tremble at the names of diseases, death in the Bibles was not terrifying. The saddest losses were often adorned with poetry. When two young sisters, Elizabeth and Mary Perkins, died on September 12, 1829, their father wrote, "They were lovely and pleasant in their lives, and in their death were not divided. Departed ones," he continued, quoting verse,

> I do not wish you here,
> But though ye are in a lovelier land,
> Among a sacred and a holy band,
> For you is yet shed many a bitter tear.

Unlike the accounts one hears of friends who are dying, the comments and remembrances in the Bibles were reassuring. My grandfather Pickering died when I was small, and although I have often heard he was a gentle, kindly man, I remember little about him except that he grew marvelous strawberries. He sold insurance, and his office was above the bank. Eight years after his death, a note appeared on the editorial page of the *Carthage Courier*. I found the note in a Bible, and it made me happy, not bringing cold and disorder to mind, but long neat rows of red strawberries. "An unprepossessing, probably little noticed metal sign, its enamel chipped with age," the note said, "is fastened to the stairway entrance of a business building here, proclaiming to his friends in life, the destiny of a man in eternity. The sign reads:

SAM PICKERING
UPSTAIRS."

Rummaging through the old books enabled me to identify some people. A little girl about eight years old and dressed completely in white from highbuttoned shoes and stockings to the ribbon in her hair was Alice Garthright, my great-grandmother. During the Battle of Cold Harbor, her home was turned into a Union hospital. The blood, so the family story goes, dripped from floor to floor and gathered in pools in the basement. Stories about the Civil War abound in my family, and I found much that touched on the conflict. When fighting broke out, my great-grandfather joined the Ohio Volunteer Infantry and fought in Kentucky and Tennessee. An older brother, Levi, was killed at Perryville, and an obituary of a younger brother, Joseph, recalled that "a memory of war days was his capture by General Stonewall Jackson at Harper's Ferry, when Jackson was storming through the Shenandoah Valley." Great-grandfather became adjutant of the Fifth Tennessee Cavalry. At the end of the war, he was stationed at Carthage, where he married and settled. After the war people collected photographs of generals, much as children collect baseball cards today. Many of the albums must have come from the Pickerings. Although one contained pictures of Robert E. Lee and Jefferson Davis, in most a headquarters of Union generals appeared: Grant,

Sherman, Thomas, O. M. Mitchell, Hooker, Rosecrans, McPherson, Butler, and Crook, all taken from negatives in Brady's National Portrait Gallery and published by E. & H. T. Anthony, 501 Broadway, New York.

I did not linger over the generals. Even pictures of great-grandfather in uniform and what must have been members of his troop did not attract my attention so much as photographs of unknown Confederates. Not only does success gradually fade into the ordinary and thus become uninteresting, but the elation of triumph so overwhelms other feelings that celebratory photographs rarely appeal to the imagination. Instead of reflecting a tapestry of emotions, such photographs only capture the simple brightness of success. Rarely do they hint at the dark complexity of life and provoke wonder. In wonder is the stuff, perhaps not of thought but of sentiment—sentiment that smooths the edges of time and turns loss into gain, making the defeated more human and more appealing than the victorious. As deaths, not births, in family Bibles attracted me, so the losers drew me, and I searched for glimpses of their lives. Little things turned up: from a desk in the attic first a bit with "7TH VA CAV CSA" stamped on it and then a single letter dated "February 16th 1864." "My Dearest Maggie," Mollie began,

> I have intended replying to your welcome affectionate letter ever since its reception but have company staying with me all the time & parties &c engrossing all time. I had rather have had a quiet time all my own in which I could have written long letters to loved friends, yet we owe certain duties to society & when there is any gayety we generally are constantly occupied. We have had a great many parties dinners &c . . . I am becoming I very much fear too dissipated. We have 8 or 10 companies of Cavalry in the county. The Regiment to which my Brother is attached is now at home, & he is with us. I was at a large dancing party, given by the Signal Corps, which is stationed a short distance from us. My Brother, a

Capt. friend from one of the R——D [Richmond] Howitzers & my sister accompanied me. I danced until 4-1/2 o'clock & got home just before day.

The dancing would not last. In less than a month Grant would take command of the Union forces. Leading the Army of the Potomac through the Wilderness, Spotsylvania Court House, Cold Harbor, and Petersburg, he drove Lee to Appomattox and surrender in April 1865. In February 1864, though, the Army of the Potomac had not crossed the Rapidan, and the dancers played. "The Capt.," Mollie wrote,

> staid with us ten days & we had many invitations out. Then I had a young lady staying here. One Saturday we went up to see a Tournament. There were eleven Knights, dressed in pretty & very becoming costumes. The cavalry had a dinner & dance on the same day & all passed pleasingly. I was invited to another party a few days since & two nice beaux came to take me but I declined. Thursday I am invited to a "grand Military Ball," given by the soldiers, several hundred invitations issued. I expect to go. Most of the girls will dress in silks. They expect a fine time. A Cousin of mine will dress in black velvet & pearls. She is a beauty & will look superbly. I will accompany her. I see some of Col. Robbins Command some times. They are stationed about 20 miles from us & have amusing dances some times. Mr. Tomkins looks so well. The Sargt has not yet returned & when asked by Mr. T—— when he would do so, his reply was by singing "When the Spring time comes gentle Annie."

Major Robinson, Mollie wrote, "is the general heart-breaker of this community. I hope I will pass unscathed." There were breaks between dances and after songs and tournaments, and Mollie was not unmarked. "Maggie dear," she concluded, "is there any appearance of peace in R——d? Do they express any hopes as to the termination of this most evil & unnatural struggle? Oh! when will we be at peace. It seems so long to look forward to—perhaps years—long weary years may escape & those most cherished will find a soldiers grave. Oh! Maggie what an awful thought! & is such a time a season for gayety—I feel condemned."

The life my great-grandfather lived in Carthage, a small town on the edge of the Cumberland Plateau, was far different from that of northern Virginia. The wife he married there was the daughter of a blacksmith, James McClarin, who after emigrating from Ireland had made his way south from Pennsylvania and who, as someone wrote beside his name in a family Bible, was known as Pittsburg Jim. His daughter Eliza Jane was not beautiful. Because she wore a brooch containing a photograph of Great-grandfather, I identified her. Her lips were narrow, and her mouth cut straight across her face. Her cheeks were thin; and her hair, twisted in small curls, was plastered down over her forehead. Her nose, too big for her mouth and cheeks, was masculine and domineering. There were no pearls or velvet, just the brooch, a white collar, and a plain checked dress. Named William Blackstone after the legal scholar, perhaps my great-grandfather wasn't interested in gaiety. When the music stopped in 1865, he was on the winning, and the right, side. Among the old books in the library was the "Memorial Record" of his funeral in 1919. The Good Samaritans–Colored Society sent flowers. "These flowers," the accompanying card stated, "are sent in grateful remembrance by the descendants of Slaves you helped to free. They will ever remember that through all the intervening years you have been their faithful guide and friend. May thy slumbers be peaceful and thy awakening pleasant in the arms of a liberty loving God."

The scrapbooks contained many photographs of the descendants of slaves: Bessie, Wilna, Mealy, Lizzie, Marie, and John Derrycote bigger than a barn and carrying me on his shoulders. Writing about these photographs is difficult, and I would like to turn from them as I did Father's love letters. Would that I could always see the springtime of my life through a haze. Age and its consort, knowledge, have, however, burned off the mist, and although I want to remember the hours spent with servants as forever golden, I have learned better and feel sick at heart when I think of seventy-year-old men calling a six-year-old boy "Mister Sammy." Among family papers was the will of Philip Claud, a distant cousin. Claud's will was made out in Williamson County, Tennessee, in April 1845. Claud seems to have owned quite a bit of property. To his daughter Matilda he bequeathed "the following negroes, to wit Wiley and Evaline"; to his son Eldridge he left Amy; to William, another son, "a negro boy named Joe"; and to Frances, a daughter, "a negro boy Anthony and a negro girl Phillis." Caroline, William, Mary, Clarissa, Sandra, Sarah, Martha, and Felise were left to other members of the family. "It is also my will and desire," Claud added, "that any increase of the above named slaves may have hereafter shall be considered and taken as bequeathed with their mothers."

In 1885 a relative in Kentucky discussed the Civil War in a letter. "It may be that Providence," he wrote, "was working out a great problem, the freedom of the negro race—which no doubt in the End, will be the best thing for us, both as a People & as a Nation!" When I was a child, the end was not in sight. Even now when I read about velvet and pearls, hear stories about my grandmother's grandmother playing the piano while field hands stood outside the parlor window singing hymns, when I recall plucking chickens in a tub of steaming hot water with Mealy, walking with Lizzie to her home in Frogtown, and driving with Grandfather to the Voodoo Man to get a hex removed from the dairy—when such things come to me, liberty and right are far out of mind. In a family Bible published in 1726, just the book of Luke was marked. A thin black line ran down the margin alongside selected verses, but only verse 20 from chapter 15, recounting the history of the Prodigal Son, was underlined.

For someone the verse was important because two thick lines underscored it. "But when he was a great way off," Luke recounted, "his father saw him, and had compassion, and ran, and fell on his neck, and kissed him." My memory is prodigal, reveling in recollections of childhood spent with the descendants of the people for whom Great-grandfather fought but who still needed, if not a guide, at least a hand toward greater freedom. Unlike the Prodigal Son, who turned his back on faraway places and returned home to lead a good life of right deeds, I left home. Memories that should have made me struggle for decency, if not justice, became artifacts, stripped of meaning and posed like holiday photographs.

Like prints sliced from an ancient folio, then framed in gold leaf and hung in an airy reception room above green plants and an Empire table, servants have appeared in my writings as parts of a decorous and soothingly smooth whole. Maybe I am too hard on myself. Like photographs, memories are packed away in sugar chests and brought out, for the most part, when it is convenient. Memories that make people uncomfortable or threaten propriety are discarded or buried deep in an attic of the mind. Days filled with uncomfortable memories become unlivable; people struggle to order and dignify their lives. Perhaps they are wise to banish indecorous Christmas cards, indeed, indecorous and disturbing thoughts. After the war William Blackstone became clerk of the county court, chief clerk of the Tennessee legislature, and then postmaster. "He filled all these positions," his obituary noted, "with unusual accuracy, care, and neatness, and wrote a splendid hand." For me, feeling vulnerable and thinking more about death and its effect upon my young children, neatness occasionally seems all important.

Tucked in among the Bibles was *Familiar Scenes; or, The Scientific Explanation of Common Things*. "I began this book in Mr. Morris School," my grandfather wrote and on the back binding listed nine students attending the school in 1885: himself, Ada Salter, Josie Myers, Charles McClarin, three Sanders children, and Ernest and Julia Fisher. At the top of page 5 he wrote,

> If how to be rich,
> you wish to find,
> look on page 109.

Immediately I turned to page 109 and read, "*Mind your business.*" The advice was good, but no Pickering, so far as I know, has ever followed it closely. At least none have been wealthy. Maybe one of my boys will, but I doubt it. If they resemble me, they will spend too much time rummaging through the past and other people's lives to mind any business. I have brought all the old family photographs, letters, books, and Bibles to Connecticut. Those that are not framed or on my bookshelves are packed in trunks in the attic. On top of the material in one trunk is an envelope that slipped out of a scrapbook and fell to the bottom of the sugar chest. Stamped on it is the return address of Grandfather's business: "Pickering & Highers Insurance, Carthage, Tennessee." Inside are copies of the Christmas cards Vicki and I have sent. To please Mother I have decided to pose in a coat and tie next year. In the future some member of the family will look at the cards. I wonder if he will notice differences in dress. I hope so, because I am going to wear the coat and tie more for him than for Mother.

Getting It

At my age there isn't much that a person gets that is good. About the best one can hope for is to slip quietly and unobtrusively through time, praying that disease and disaster won't notice him. Life did not begin this way. Years ago dreams warmed my days like the morning sun, and possibilities rang through the night like song. As a small boy I read a bookshelf of inspirational biographies about young Americans. Bound in orange and published by Bobbs-Merrill, the books pointed the way to success and indeed immortality, teaching that nothing lay beyond the grasp of the plucky and the industrious. Through impenetrable forest and desolate plain I wandered with *Daniel Boone, Boy Hunter* and *Meriwether Lewis, Boy Explorer.* With *The Mill Boy of the Slashes,* Henry Clay, I went to Washington. I was beside *Sam Houston, Boy Chieftain* when he caught Santa Anna napping and brought Texas into the land of the free and the deserving. With Wilbur and Orville Wright, *Boys with Wings,* I escaped mortal gravity and, soaring above dull earth, imagined the future bright before me like a giant apple tree, its fruits red and juicy, just waiting for me, and me alone, to pick them.

I soon learned better. Instead of beacons lighting the way to achievement, the biographies resembled the will o' the wisp, drawing youth into a wasteland pocked with disappointment. And those apples that seemed so fair in the sunny pages of biography often proved green and wormeaten, and bitter to the taste. Not that I actually ate many. Visions rarely include practicalities like ladders and bushel baskets, and I have spent most of my adult years at the feet of trees, hands empty and tasting fruits only in my imagination. This, however, is not a state to be lamented; indeed, not getting what one dreams about may be one of life's great blessings.

Girls—silly, laughing girls—first taught me that getting what I wanted was going to be impossible. In the 1960s I was a student at Cambridge University. Tom Henn, my tutor, had extraordinarily broad interests and had written books on Yeats, poetry and painting, fishing, and German small arms. Although old and partially crippled, Tom coached one of the college crews. When I knew him, he was particularly drawn to myth and folktale. When tutorial discussions drifted toward the abstract, he brought them back to red clay, interrupting to recount a bawdy or horrifically violent story. For him boys became men on the river or on the battlefield or in the bedroom, anywhere, it seemed, but in class, and on my arrival in Cambridge, he urged me to forget books, saying, "Mr. Pickering, if you wanted to be a scholar, you should have stayed in the United States." I attempted to follow his advice but, as a bookish person, was not very successful. Still, I tried, rowing and playing water polo. One week I was so busy that I neglected to prepare an assigned essay. The simple, and true, statement that I had not planned my time well sounded priggish and would not have pleased Tom. Something more lively was called for.

"Mr. Henn," I said on entering his rooms, "I am sorry but I have not done this week's essay. I have had," I said pausing, "a problem with a brown-eyed woman."

"Well, well," Tom exclaimed heartily and, heaving himself out of his chair, put his arm across my shoulders and said, "Sam, I hope you have many more problems just like her."

I didn't. Not writing the essay was out of character. I was a good student and followed instructions meticulously, always taking *no* for *no* and *don't* for *don't*. Most of the time I never bothered to ask the question, but simply assumed the answer would be *no*. I was the sort of boy who, when a girl I was visiting in France called me into her bedroom and asked me to zip up the back of her dress, did—woe is me—exactly that. Even on those rare occasions when I pulled the zipper south rather than north, I later regretted it. My first real love after Cambridge was Sophy. I loved her with all the impetuosity of youth and pursued her with an energy foreign to my experience. For a while Sophy paid little attention but then she bent and invited me to spend Christmas with her and her family in Wisconsin. Late at night after her parents were safely asleep, Sophy crept out of her room, tiptoed down the long hall, and knocked softly at my door. One night while she was with me, her mother called from the kitchen. In a flash she was out of the bed and through the door. All I wanted was to pull the covers over my head in hopes the bed would become an enchanted cave out of which I could crawl and find myself safely back home in Tennessee. Alas, enchanted caves and magical doors are found only in children's books. Getting up and putting on my bathrobe, I went to the door and listened. From the kitchen, I heard the murmur of voices; then Sophy began to cry. Her tears soaked through her nightgown to my conscience. "By God," I thought, "I am just as responsible as she is. I can't let her take the blame by herself." With that I pulled my bathrobe tight and strode out of the bedroom and down the stairs into the kitchen. Determined to do the decent thing, I did not notice the puzzled expressions on the faces of Sophy and her mother.

"Sam, what . . ." Sophy began.

"Be quiet," I barked; "let me handle this. Mrs. Currer," I said and, tolerating no interruption, shouldered responsibility for

Sophy's nightly visits. "Don't blame Sophy," I said; "she didn't want to come, but I told her if she loved me, she wouldn't stay away."

"That," Mrs. Currer said after I finished, "is extremely interesting, but I wasn't talking to Sophy about that. I called her to tell her her great uncle Sven died."

I wish I could say the evening in the kitchen took away my appetite for the things of this world. Unfortunately, hot youth finds it difficult to diet. Although I felt uncomfortable and was slightly down in the mouth when I sat down to breakfast the next morning, I was hungry. Stoutheartedly I took on the grapefruit, eggs, sausage, potatoes, biscuits and jam, and then the home-made apple pie that Mrs. Currer put before me. The food bucked me up considerably, and by the end of the meal, I had almost forgotten the embarrassment of the night before. Indeed, and I am ashamed to say it now, breakfast only whetted my appetites, and as I sat there, talking about the cold Wisconsin winter and sipping coffee, all I could think about was biting into soft, warm Sophy. Although Sophy gave me the it I thought I wanted as a callow youth, I never really got her, and by the next Christmas she had drifted away, leaving me feeling more alone than I ever felt in that Wisconsin kitchen.

Years and the time for mongrel love have passed. Countless disappointments and embarrassments have taught me the danger of pursuing anything. Still, humans are frail and in the passion of a moment often forget lessons driven home by hard experience. On weekends I run road races. I am remarkably slow, and in the four years I have been running seriously have not won a trophy or even a ribbon. Only once have I come close. Last year I ran in Norwich during a storm. While thunder slammed above the city and water gushed out of storm drains, sensible people stayed comfortably at home. Not me—knowing that the storm would reduce the field, I realized this was the best chance I would ever have to win a trophy, and doing my utmost to ignore the rain and thunder, I slogged through the streets. At the end of the race, I appeared successful and was given a trophy for finishing third in the forty-to-fifty-year-old age group. I was elated and fondled the trophy with as much fervor as an aging, spent runner is capable. I should have known better. Like Sophy, the things we get flow so swiftly through our hands that we are often left with nothing except laughter and the wish we had never possessed them. The trophy was mine for two minutes; then, it being discovered that someone else had actually finished third in my division, I was forced to give it up.

In truth returning the trophy saved me trouble. At home finding a place for it in the study would have been difficult. After a while, it would have become a nuisance, gathering dust and liable to be knocked over and broken by my little boys. Indeed, those things people work for, our possessions—both material goods and the immaterial past like memories of Sophy—weigh life down. That mark of success, a large house, doesn't bring pleasure. The bigger the house, the more pipes there are to burst, the more plaster to crack, the more wallpaper for children to peel off. My house has a big front yard, and friends say I am fortunate to have it for the children to play in. I am not sure. The grass not being so green as I wanted it, this spring I spent fifty-two dollars and thirty-four cents on fertilizer. Now I have the best crop of weeds in the neighborhood. Mowing accomplishes little; overnight the weeds seem to spring knee high, and now I have to buy weedkiller. Once the weeds are dead, I will harrow up the yard, rake, scatter grass seed, and cover everything with straw. Then watering begins. During the whole process, the children won't be allowed to play on the lawn.

Summer will come and go, and the children will be inside. At least they will be there if I and the things I worked so hard to get can stand them. Last week I almost had a fit when my two-year-old son, Edward, broke a cedar and mother-of-pearl footstool I had purchased in the Mideast. A decade ago I spent a year in Jordan. I bought many things, and on leaving shipped four large crates, 450 pounds' worth of possessions, to Tennessee. On their way the crates went astray. Little Edward's life, and probably mine too, would be more tranquil if they had not turned up. Unhappily for Edward, I determined to get what, I said, was mine. The crates left Jordan on Alia, the Jordanian national airline, on the same day in early June that I left. I did not fly directly home but spent the summer in London working in the British Library. When I arrived in Tennessee in early September, I was astonished and irritated to learn that my freight was not there. Father traced it to New York, where Eastern Airlines had taken possession on the seventeenth of June. For a month and a half he had struggled to trace it farther. The Eastern representative in Nashville was polite but ineffectual, assuring Father "that we are doing the best we can." Upset, I sent a registered letter to the president of Eastern. Although I am a poor typist, I typed the letter myself on nondescript stationery. Three weeks passed, and then an answer arrived. The airline was unimpressed, and the man who responded was condescending rather than apologetic or accommodating. Instead of assuring me that the company would do its best to locate my possessions, he briskly requested a list of everything in the crates. At this point I should have stopped. Alas, I did not. The father of one of my closest friends was chairman of the board of a large corporation. Each year his company sent hundreds of employees to a combination convention-vacation. All the employees traveled on Eastern charter flights. The company did so much business with Eastern that the president of the airlines himself came to Nashville to meet my friend's father and spent two days as his houseguest. Upon learning this, I sent another registered letter to the president of Eastern. This time I had a professional type it on formal university letterhead stationery. Near the end was a paragraph reading, "Cormac Leighton, chairman of the board of such-and-such corporation, asked me to send you his regards. He requests that you personally look into the matter of my air freight. Anything you could do to facilitate this would be greatly appreciated." Five days later a van pulled into the driveway. In the back was my air freight, those possessions that have bothered me ever since, making moving difficult and now threatening to bedevil the lives of my children. People who strive after things often get the unexpected. Along with my possessions, I received a knowledge of influence and the workings of the world, and it left a sour taste in my mouth, one that I have never been able to wash away completely.

When I was a graduate student, I rarely participated in class discussions. Seminars were the curse of my days. Most of the talk was beyond me, and when it wasn't, it bounced so quickly from topic to topic that I was always panting far behind. No matter how well I prepared I could not keep up, and as the class steadily pulled away, leaving me stumbling and blind in a cloud of intellectual dust, I used to pray, "Oh, Lord, give me an idea. Don't make me appear such an ignoramus." My prayers must have gotten lost in the high, white ether and could not make it to heaven, for I never got an idea, at least not one I could articulate. In retrospect, I suppose I was fortunate. Not being a chosen vessel, academic or religious, one of those winged students on whom professors pin bright hopes and to whom they devote close attention, I remained comparatively free. Rather than struggling after the good things of academic life, prestigious jobs or influential editorships, I took the little bits that fell my way. And, lo, much like the miracle of the loaves and fishes, the bits have been endlessly satisfying. Instead of laboring through rain and thunder in pursuit of glitter, I have remained snug at home. Although I have won none of the trophies of the profession, grants and fellowships, I have experienced little disappointment. Perhaps my prayers made it through the pearly gates after all and have been answered—although not in the way I hoped but in the way that was best for me.

"No, my friend, you have got things wrong," an ambitious acquaintance responded when I talked to him about my career. Maybe I am incorrect, but getting things wrong often strikes me as better than getting them right. Certainly in the classroom a wrong answer is often more entertaining and memorable than a right answer. In an essay my students read recently the word *bordello* appeared.

"Steve," I asked, "what's a bordello?"

"It's," he said, "a kind of cheese, isn't it?"

Wrong, but yet bordello ought to be a cheese, wedged between the imported and the domestic, alongside the Stilton and the cheddar. Getting right answers or attaining goals too often ends things. The pleasure in getting things or having goals, be they trophies or Sophys, lies not in achievement but in anticipation. In ending the Uncle Wiggily stories, Howard Garis understood this well. What appealed to children was not the next night's story so much as it was what might happen during the day. "Now," a tale typically concluded, "if our cook makes some nice watermelon sandwiches, with maple syrup on them, for supper, I'll tell you tomorrow night about Uncle Wiggily and old dog Percival, and why Percival cried."

For my part, I don't want to know why Percival cried. Better it may be to leave tears and laughter shrouded in mystery. The attempt to get at the truth or to discover reasons for behavior is often destructive. Explanations and speculation frequently lessen life. Mr. Fenik was a handyman on my grandfather's dairy farm in Virginia. He and his wife lived in a small house behind Grandfather's garage. While Mr. Fenik was at work, Mrs. Fenik tended a garden she planted along the edge of a field near her home. She was a fine gardener, and by late summer the garden was a wonderfully green place overflowing with cantaloupes, watermelons, beefsteak tomatoes, squash, cucumbers, corn, snaps, radishes, and onions. More than anything else Mrs. Fenik loved butterbeans, and down through the middle of the garden ran four long rows like a great hedge. The Feniks were an affectionate couple, and if they had not been addicted to drink would have led a conventional life. On warm nights when she had too much to drink, Mrs. Fenik went into the garden. She always wore a blue nightgown and invariably went to the butterbean patch. Squatting down under the poles with the vines hanging about her, she sang hymns: "Bringing in the Sheaves," "Whispering Hope," and, amazingly enough, the occasional temperance hymn—"O Rouse Ye, Christian Women" or "Drink Water Every One."

Along one side of the garden grew a clump of dwarf cedar trees. Once we heard Mrs. Fenik start to sing, my cousin Sherry and I would sneak out of grandfather's house and crawl under a tree and listen. The butterbeans were so thick that seeing Mrs. Fenik was difficult, and although we could guess where she was from her singing, we rarely saw her. When we did, Mr. Fenik was responsible. After his wife had been in the butterbean patch for a while, he frequently appeared. Instead, though, of going into the garden, he stopped at the edge and, picking up clumps of loose dirt, lobbed them high into the air above Mrs. Fenik and the butterbeans. Occasionally the clumps fell on her and Mrs. Fenik squealed and, jumping about, darted to a new spot in the patch. For a person who had been drinking, she moved quickly, and we had to be alert to get even a glimpse of her nightgown in the moonlight.

For four summers Mrs. Fenik sang and Mr. Fenik threw dirt; then suddenly they stopped. Just beyond the garden the field sloped down to a gully; across the gully grew two weeping willow trees. One dry September night while Mrs. Fenik was singing and the wind blew across the gully and over the garden, Mr. Fenik went to his car. From the trunk he took a chain saw and a can of gasoline; this time instead of stopping at the edge of the garden, he pushed through and down across the gully. There he started the saw and felled both trees. After heaping the branches into a big brushpile, he doused them with gasoline and then lit them. Immediately fire ran through the willows and sparks by the thousands flew into the air. Caught in the wind, they blew across the gully and fell like orange rain on the garden. For a moment Mrs. Fenik stopped singing and was silent; then leaping out of the butterbeans, she screamed, "Jesus," and, stumbling across the cantaloupes and the tomatoes, ran out of the garden and back into the house. Never again did Mrs. Fenik sing hymns in the garden. By the following summer she and her husband were gone, and although I have often wondered what motivated Mr. Fenik to start the fire, I have never gone beyond wonder. Why on that one night did he act so differently? What provoked him? How did the fire change the marriage? For such questions there are answers, but I don't want to know them. Instead of having the Feniks' behavior packaged and wrapped in pressed, brown explanation, then stacked upstairs in the dust beside trunks and old books, never to be thought about again, I want those summer nights to remain green, songs and butterbeans rising from the black earth, watered by a curiosity that speculates but does not dig and uproot searching for reason.

Certainly there are times when a person has to understand and understand quickly. Years ago I attended wrestling matches and cheered the villains. One evening when I was applauding the antics of two masked Japanese gentlemen who were busy pulling the hair and stomping on the hands of their fair, blue-eyed opponents, a hill of a man in overalls sitting in front of me turned around and said, "Boy, haven't you ever heard of Pearl Harbor?" Then pausing, he glared and added, "You get me?" I got him right away, and, like the song of the lark at dawn, patriotism burst forth from my lips. Beginning to scowl and muttering evil things about Iwo Jima and Guadalcanal, I cheered our boys on to victory. By the end of the evening the big man was friendly, and as we were leaving he slapped me on the back and said, "You learn fast; you are my kind of boy."

Getting things right, however, does not guarantee acceptance. More often than not it isolates, sometimes even provoking people to behave like the big man at the wrestling match. A southern acquaintance has not been friendly ever since I interrupted him once when he was talking about "good old boys." "Good old boys," I said, determined to get something right, "good old boys—so far as I can judge—are always young and bad."

Another acquaintance and I parted after a discussion of familiar sayings. "When the going gets tough, the tough get going," I told him, was painted on the wall of the locker room in my high school gymnasium.

"I know that one," he said; "it's one of the good ones. That's what made this country great: people who refused to quit. When times were hard, they showed true grit, dug in, and held on until victory."

"You've got it all wrong," I answered; "I don't know where the tough went when times became rough. But wherever it was, if they were smart, it was somewhere soft. As for sticking around and showing grit," I added, getting under a full head of truth, "the Founding Fathers of this country were quitters, or at least their daddies and granddaddies were. Americans quit other countries by the wheelbarrow and came here hoping the going would not be so tough and they could start new lives in a good soft spot."

No, getting things right or even getting the things I think about is not for me. For years I have struggled not to want things and have asked family to refrain from buying presents on Christmas and my birthday. Besides, clothes are about the only thing people give folks my age, and I am not a sartorial high-flyer. Moreover, as a teacher I don't need much in my closet. Over twenty years ago, in June 1964 to be exact, James Neal of 71 and 72 Trumpington Street in Cambridge made the jacket I wear to most classes. In winter I wear corduroy trousers and in summer Sears Perma-Prest. Twelve years ago a relative gave me a box of J. C. Penney shirts, 80 per cent Dacron polyester and 20 per cent combed cotton. The shirts are indestructible and are for all seasons. This is not to say that I don't have a couple of affectations. On sunny summer and spring days, I wear a sailor's hat, brim turned permanently down, manufactured by Derby Cap Company of Louisville, Kentucky. When my students see me, they say things like, "Here comes Gilligan's Island." About every sixteen months or so, I lose my cap, and Santa Claus then knows what to put in his bag for me that Christmas.

Of course, no matter how one fights, a person cannot completely stifle desire. Sometimes after a long and dark day, I dream of meeting Sophy again. Occasionally when I can't sleep, cold years drip away like ice in March, and I imagine her tiptoeing down the hall and slipping into my room. Unlike youthful hopes, however, this is a dream that I pray will never come true. Getting caught now would lead to worse than embarrassment and take more than appetite away. Happy in the bright day, surrounded by family and all the little business of family life, I don't think much about the past, and my one or two waking dreams pertain to the future. I write familiar essays, and I imagine receiving wondrous mail. "After reading your splendid story," my imaginary letter begins, "I have decided you are the very one. Enclosed you will find a check. I hope it will be sufficient for you to take your family away to some exotic place for a year and devote your energies, full time, to your next book." Not surpisingly, the check is more than enough, and within a month the Pickerings are winging their way—and winging it first class—to Patmos or the Seychelles.

I receive quite a bit of mail, but none of it ever contains a check. Still, even though I don't get what I dream about, I do get marvelous letters. Filled with unexpected delightfully odd statements, the letters carry me to lands, I sometimes think, that Meriwether Lewis, the boy explorer, never imagined. Just yesterday two wonderful letters arrived. "As a lifetime academic" a woman wrote in analyzing one of my essays, "I also resonate to your subtext." What she meant I have no idea, but my speculations had me flying higher and farther than those boys with wings. Accompanying the second letter was a book written by Annalee Skarin, who, the editor's note assured readers, did not die but "underwent a physical change known as 'translation,' such as did Enoch of Biblical days." A man who read a piece of mine on turtles sent the book. Although the book was "not overtly relevant to that article," he sent it to me "after seeking Divine guidance on the matter." Able to communicate with the Great First Cause, the man would not have been at a loss for words in one of my graduate seminars.

Six weeks ago Eliza McClarin Pickering was born. She is her daddy's little dreamboat; unfortunately at night she does not flow out with the tide and dream. Instead she stays up, and has a fine time gurgling and kicking. The only thing that puts her to sleep is my singing to her. My voice isn't as good as that of Mrs. Fenik, but my repertoire is larger: "Good-Night Irene," "The Downtown Strutters' Ball," "Tennessee Waltz," "The Halls of Montezuma," "Battle Hymn of the Republic," "Yellow Rose of Texas," and "Daisy." I even sing hymns: "Faith of Our Fathers," "Onward Christian Soldiers," "From Greenland's Icy Mountains." What I sing most, however, is Stephen Foster. Alas, gone are the days when my memory was young and good, and I have forgotten the words to many of his songs. As I pace back and forth across the bedroom, cradling Eliza, I find myself wishing for an album of Stephen Foster so I could get the words and sometimes tunes down right. Such a wish seems simple enough and likely to cause fewer problems than most of the things for which I once wished. Unfortunately, that is just not so. I don't own a record player, and if I bought one on which to play a Stephen Foster album, I don't know where I would put it so the boys could not reach it. If I bought an expensive record player and Edward broke it, I would be furious and probably behave worse than Mr. Fenik with his chain saw.

Country Life

Good country people scare the hell out of me. Once I liked the country and thought that the closer a person was to the soil the nearer he was to God. I know better now. The closer a person is to the soil the dirtier he is. Heaven is far above earth, and only by keeping sin from soiling him can a man get a handhold on Jacob's ladder and pull himself off the ground. Romanticizing country life is simpleminded. Instead of digging down to roots, families should look up to flowers. The flower is a long way from the root, and it takes generations, usually five or six cultivated ones, before a family blooms.

Open fields make me shudder. People and gardens grow behind walls. In a garden weeds can be poisoned and a lawn rolled flat. In a field blackberries pull at clothes and animal runs make walking dangerous. I haven't always thought this way, though; when I was a child in Virginia I enjoyed exploring and disliked boundaries, believing they fenced off the unpredictable beauty of the world. Each warm summer night, my friends and I played a game called "No Bears." The boy who was the bear hid in a lane of blue cedars along a road. After he disappeared, the rest of us crept off from the base, my grandfather's bright front porch, and wandered into the dark chanting, "No bears are out tonight; no bears are out tonight." When the bear decided we were too far from the porch to get back easily, he leapt out of hiding and, roaring loudly, tried to catch one of us. In part we enjoyed the game because we knew no real bears were nearby. Of course we were wrong; youth kept us from realizing that all sorts of bears lurked in the shadows not simply beyond the porch but within ourselves. When I last heard from Raymond, the best bear among us, he was in prison for armed robbery.

Two of my country friends were named Peter Rabbit and Moccasin Snake. How wonderful it would be, I used to think, to have a name like theirs, and in daydreams, I shed dull Sam for June Bug, Polecat, and Terrapin. Now, instead of attracting, such names repel me as I labor through days searching for modest, proper words and through years trying to live the right, quiet way. Rather than appearing creatively alive, colorful names seem frightening emblems of the breakdown of civility and order. Man, not nature, imposes propriety on life, and in the open country tares choke even the beauty of budding women given lovely names like Osceola, Eulalia, and Estelle. When she was young, Libbyrose, the daughter of one of our laborers, seemed greenly natural, but then unpruned freedom took her promise. She married young and blew before she blossomed.

Thought often undermines action, and success may depend upon not finding meaning in daily life. Although living in the country strips life almost to myth, it does not provide tools with which to interpret existence. Only behind walls does a person learn to find meaning; happily, such meaning resembles play and rarely influences living unless one strays into the country. There meaning soon becomes unbearable. Wallace Johnson was the only son of a widow, and although he could not speak, he could moo like a cow. Every afternoon just as storm clouds began to roll along the nearby river and the cows turned toward the barn to be milked, Wallace walked up our road. When he reached the fence that separated pasture from yard, he took the barbed wire in his hands and then, looking at the cows, mooed until they disappeared. The wire cut his hands and his palms were covered with scars. Wallace's mother tried to make him wear gloves, but he always lost them. Wallace died when he was twenty-eight, and I missed him. He was a curious and entertaining part of my afternoons; I laughed when he mooed and tried to see his hands. Occasionally I found a glove on our road and took it to Mrs. Johnson, who gave me candy or treated me to cake and a glass of milk. Today I don't miss Wallace; only at night do I think about him. Then he appears, his hands red and his mouth open and full of sound.

Walls protect people from raw emotions and make a thoughtful existence possible. As one listens to Liszt or Schubert at a memorial service, Death seems a courtier. In the country there are funerals, not memorial services, and Death does not carry people off on the wings of melody but tears them away through tears. The funeral of Wilna, Grandfather's cook, was held in a little country church. The congregation was poor and could not afford an organ. When the funeral began, a big man stood and in a voice that seemed to fall from heaven sang "Nearer My God to Thee." Instead of transporting the congregation to another safer time and place, the hymn pushed people closer to God and they began to weep. In his sermon, the preacher told us that when Wilna died a fiery chariot traveled across the sky. "Daughter," a voice said; and when Wilna answered, "Here I am, Lord," a burning hand softer than new milk reached down and took her into the chariot. "Oh, Mister Sam," Mealy said as we stood outside the church, "that sermon had real gravy in it." Yes, the sermon did have real gravy, full of the rich fat of life. But now that I live far from the country, I eat health foods and avoid things that cause heart pain.

In being part of the rhythm of birth and death, life has little value in the country; only behind walls do fictions about the sanctity and worth of the individual seem true. For an evening in June, Grandfather planned a party in the garden. Early that afternoon there was a thunderstorm. Lightning struck locust trees in the yard and branches fell across boxwoods, opening them like cakes that cooked too long. Grandfather sent for Mr. Harkins, a laborer who often worked in the garden. It was a long time before Mr. Harkins came. When he appeared, he apologized and explained that his nephew had drowned in the river. "I told him to stay away from the river," he said, "but he just wouldn't listen." Then without saying anything else, he got a saw and some baling wire from the tool shed. He climbed the locust trees and cut off the broken limbs and then mended the boxwoods with the wire. I raked up the twigs, and by the time the guests arrived, no one could tell there had been a storm.

Laborers like Mr. Harkins never stayed long on the farm. They lived in a row of small frame houses near the dairy, and whenever a family left, I went to the house to see what I could find. The houses were similar and discouraging. On a wall was a calendar with a picture of Jesus on it. Scattered about the floor were coathangers and old shoes, always missing laces and down at the heel. Bits of cardboard were patched across cracked window panes, and in the back yard were tires, tin cans, and broken toys. Only in a walled-in world do the remnants of primitive living become interesting. Suspended over my breakfast table is a battered nineteenth-century weathervane shaped like a snake. The kitchen doorstop is a wrought iron scraper, while along a wall sits a crudely painted blanket chest of yellow pine. Hanging from an old coach jack above it is a crewel embroidered bed covering depicting birds waking up in a cherry tree. By themselves these pieces of other lives are dead and teach that all man's possessions, and indeed accomplishments, like those things left behind in the houses on Grandfather's farm, ultimately become trash. Yet behind walls, far from the country and the times which produced them, these remnants live. Instead of discouraging, they encourage by showing that not only can man escape primitive living but that by artistically arranging the refuse of simple life he can create a cleaner, sophisticated world.

"Keep your eyes peeled," Mealy said whenever I went outside the house, "there is no telling what you might see." As a country child I saw many things: turkey buzzards in a corn field fighting over a litter of drowned kittens, copperheads in a woodshed, and cicadas breaking through their shells and pushing out wet and silver onto trees. One day as I walked along the train tracks that ran from Richmond to Fredericksburg, I saw a cloud of tiger swallowtail butterflies fluttering about pink mullein. Hanging on the plants and looking just like leaves were myriads of praying mantises, and whenever a butterfly lit, a mantis seized it and quickly ate the body, letting the wings fall to the ground. For a hundred yards, the ground seemed covered with yellow snow, and I ran laughing along the tracks, kicking my feet through the wings and throwing handfuls above my head.

Occasionally I see butterflies now, but I have not seen a praying mantis for years. I have worked hard, not so much to avoid seeing, but to escape actuality by transforming what is seen, or experienced, into something else. In the country transformations do not come easily, and praying mantises hang upside down on plants, still and green as leaves waiting for butterflies. When Willie Atwood, one of Grandfather's laborers, drank, he beat his wife and children. One night he seized his wife by the hair and threw her so fiercely across the room that her head smashed through the wallboard. My friend Bartlip, Willie's twelve-year-old son, then took a stick from the woodbox and knocked his father unconscious, after which he and his mother and the other children ran to us and asked to spend the night. When Willie came to, he went after his friend Henry Madger. After drinking more, they loaded their shotguns and started hunting Bartlip. For most of the night they stumbled through the pasture and crashed through the boxwoods in the yard, shooting and yelling things like "There goes the little son of a bitch!" Grandfather didn't call the sheriff that night because he said if he did someone would probably be shot. Eventually Willie and Henry collapsed in the yard, and early in the morning Grandfather called the sheriff. He came and took their guns away and locked them up for two days. When he got out, Willie felt guilty, and the next time he drank, he knocked at the back door and asked for Grandfather. "Mr. Ratcliffe," he said, "I've got five dollars; let's go to Richmond and have a big time." Grandfather thanked Willie but turned down the invitation. When Grandfather told us about it, we laughed. Not long afterward, Willie and his family moved on. His invitation, however, stayed behind; and whenever we started for Richmond, someone was sure to say, "I've got five dollars; let's have a big time."

For a few months Bartlip was my best friend, and although I smiled whenever one of my family alluded to his father, I have never been quite able to forget or transform his history into comfortable humor. As I watch my son grow while I slowly age, jealousy and anger take seed within me, and I wonder if I will ever hunt him, not with a gun but with piercing criticism. By turning country things into words, perhaps I can wall out my life in the country and that country that lies within me. Some memories, alas, lie beyond mortar and words: a hot day in a pine woods when two boys took off their clothes and demonstrated "cornholing" and a cold Christmas noon after I sent trinkets to some poor children and their proud father made them give me the few nice toys they had received. Still, if I stay behind walls and arrange the fragments of country life artistically, perhaps I will never think about such things again and my son will bloom far from those roots that pull him toward the ground.

Moving On
_____

"My wife's relatives are gregarious and nomadic," Mr. Crittle was fond of saying. Each year when the Pedigrift tribe migrated to Carthage, Mr. Crittle closed his insurance office and moved into the Grand Hotel in Red Boiling Springs. No catastrophe, no number of claims could lure him away, and he stayed glued to Red Boiling Springs until the last of the Pedigrifts left Carthage. Neither appearance nor his wife's pleading counted for much with Mr. Crittle; years had taught him the wisdom of decamping when his in-laws began to arrive. Eventually, life teaches all people the virtues and the necessity of occasionally moving on. Raised on a stringy regimen of "stand fast" and "hold tight," youth, however, is not always sympathetic to the notion and often needs convincing. Until a cold, still night in Maine, I fancied myself rock hard and practically unmovable. That night as I paced down the shoulder of a road, a car full of men drew alongside. It slowed, and one of the men rolled down his window and threw a beer can at me. I was angry, and, high-stepping out to the middle of the road, I set my feet astride the pavement like the Colossus over the harbor at Rhodes and, shaking my fist, yelled, "Come back here, you sons of bitches!" I have, alas, a strong voice. The men in the car heard me, and almost, it seemed, before I stopped shouting, the car had spun around. A tidal wave of fear swept over me, and by the time the car reached the spot where I had stood, immobile and statuelike, I was deep into the woods and long gone.

Twenty-five years have passed since that night in Maine. Now cussing doesn't make me blink, or speak. Whenever I hear bad language, I behave like Mr. Crittle and depart, heading for my own Grand Hotel. There I sit, oblivious to the Pedigrifts, rocking on the porch until the evening turns blue and calm. Over the years I have moved on from many things, albeit not with the speed with which I hotfooted it through the Maine woods. At my age there is no fast lane; there may not even be a path, and in hopes of walking a little farther through the brush, I have left behind many of the appurtenances of "the good life." No longer does my house flow with drink and swell with convivial song. "My little dog" has had more than his "ears cut short and his tail cut long." He has fled cowed to the pound. No longer do I want to bring old acquaintance to mind; now I prefer the sober strains of

> Hurrah! For Sparkling Water, the cool, the pure, and the free;
> The silver plashing water, that murmurs o'er the lea;
> It gives us health and vigor, it makes us bold and strong;
> Unfurl the Temp'rance banner, and this shall be our song.

I'm not too old to cut the cheese; it's just that a full-bodied Brie has too much cholesterol for a family man. Along with spirits I have left many old friends behind, particularly those who recall Maine nights. My perspective has changed; I want my past to remain decently hidden behind sentiment. Stripped in the harsh sun of the present, good days swiftly go bad. Along with old friends I have moved on from the ambitious and the sanctified. Fervor of any sort rises like cucumbers to the heart and makes me bilious. For generations my family has lacked fervor, accomodatingly moving from church to church. In Pennsylvania and Virginia we were Quakers; in Ohio, Methodists; in Tennessee, first members of the Christian church and then Episcopalians. Next month here in Connecticut my little girl Eliza will be christened in the Congregational church.

Much of the moving on that people do is generated by others. This year a collection of my essays was published. Before the book appeared, I wrote editors urging them to review it. When I mentioned to my parents that I was writing editors, Father was chagrined.

"Without publicity," I explained, "a good book will die."

"Not all the publicity in the world," Father replied, "can prevent a bad book from committing suicide."

Father had read the manuscript and was embarrassed and apprehensive, embarrassed because the book called attention to the family and apprehensive that the attention would be unfavorable. Father believed it better to pass through life in quiet, unchronicled dignity than to publish a mediocre book. Surprisingly, the book sold. People telephoned my parents, saying the essays brought them pleasure, and Father moved on. When I visited Tennessee in January, he urged me to drum up more publicity. "A good book like this," he told me, "needs publicity or else it will die."

Moving on and leaving friends behind creates the belief that one changes for the better. That is an illusion; the truth may be that one never really moves on. Inessentials like drink can be tossed aside, but the essentials of personality remain the same. My family's shifts from the Quakers to the Methodists and then to the Episcopal church were changes in name only. For generations we have avoided zeal and adjusted ourselves to the little worlds immediately surrounding us. Differences between generations may at first appear great but usually are superficial. Wealth and education come and go, but patterns of living remain the same. This December I sent my children a letter from Santa Claus, asking what they wanted for Christmas and telling them to give their daddy a list to mail to the North Pole. "Since there were twenty million more children this year than last," I wrote, "Santa is a little short on money" and I asked them not to list every toy they could think of, "just your favorites." After Christmas during my visit in Tennessee, I found a letter my grandfather sent me forty years ago. "It is getting pretty close to Christmas," he wrote, "and Santa Claus says he will not have time to come by here to see about everything for you, so I am sending your Mother some money and she will pay for the presents when Santa Claus brings them that night. She has to pay for some of the presents because Santa Claus doesn't have the money this year that he had last year. There are almost thirteen million more children to buy something for, so you see he is having a hard time this year, but he told me that he is going to take care of your presents, so I don't think you need to worry."

From previous generations people inherit not merely patterns of living but possessions. What others leave behind silently becomes part of the fabric of our lives. Instead of moving on and furnishing a home with the new, people use the old, often making it the focal point of a room and shaping order and lives around it. Over the fireplace in my living room is a bull's eye mirror. Atop the frame is a gold eagle. With its neck twisted forward and to the side and its wings pulled back, the eagle is poised to sweep out into the room. Rarely do guests fail to notice the mirror, and it has started many conversations about possessions and the past. Often talk turns from the mirror to knickknacks beneath it on the mantelpiece. The thing which attracts most attention is an old china papboat. Shaped like an elongated cup with a thumb notch at one end and a round mouthpiece at the other, the papboat was used to feed gruel to babies in the nineteenth century. Around the outside of the cup are blue and yellow periwinkle blossoms. Inside the bowl are dark green leaves, and slender gray stems stretch down the mouthpiece. I do not know who owned the mirror and the papboat originally; yet as that person's possessions are now mine, so I am partly his.

Possessions of others have become so much the fabric of my days that I notice them only when someone calls attention to them. Just last week an acquaintance asked about a painting that hangs in the upstairs hall. During the day I pass it a score of times, but, as with inherited patterns of living, I rarely look at it. An oil painting of a dog with the name Tory painted in the lower right-hand corner, the picture has a primitive, anecdotal charm. Tory looks like a terrier. His fur sticks out like straw in all directions, and if it were not for a red nose, two black eyes, and four round, ball-like feet standing on something that resembles cobblestones slowly being hidden under a green mold, he could be mistaken for a small bale of hay. Even though the painting has no artistic merit and I rarely notice it, Tory has become so much a part of my unconscious life that if I moved to a new house, I would hang him in the upstairs hall.

Possessions possess their owner, not simply adorning his world but binding him to the past. Attempting to change their lives, people often try to divest themselves of possessions. Few succeed. In September I started to clean out my desk. Bulging with photographs, letters, notes for essays, and ends of erasers and pencils, the desk has been in my family for generations and is almost an emblem of memory, crammed with useless and sometimes embarrassing bits and pieces of the past. I got up early and, carrying a big rubber trash can into the study, attacked the desk. When I removed the top drawer so I could empty it, I noticed a piece of yellow paper stuck to the inside rear of the desk. In the 1850s, someone tore an advertisement out of a Nashville newspaper and put it in the top drawer. Other papers being tossed in afterward, the advertisement was probably pushed back in the drawer, where it slowly became gritty. One day when the drawer was jerked open, the paper must have been pulled over the top of the drawer, and, instead of falling to the floor, it must have stuck to the back of the desk. Whatever happened, though, the cleaning ended when I found the advertisement. Andrew Anderson, a brass and iron founder at "No. 53 Broad Street, near Cor. Broad and Cherry," declared that he had "a Full Supply of the Following Articles, Constantly on Hand." Anderson must have done a thriving business, because his list was full: "Coal Stoves, Grates for Coal, Mantel Grates, Grate Bars, Swedge Black, Twere Irons, Mandrales, Iron Fencing, Balconies, Steam Engines, Horse-Powers, Curry Combs, Coffee Mills, Tea Kettles, Brass Kettles, Collins' Axes, Hatchets, Coal Buckets, Candle-sticks, L. H. Shovels, Shovels and Tongs, Foot Scrapers, Wagon Boxes, Hollow Ware, Plow Moulds, Car Wheels, Straw Cutters, Corn Shellers, Corn Crushers, Little Giant, Farm Mill Irons, Mill Spindles, Mill Cranks, Mill Gudgeons, Curren Wheels, Hotchkiss Wheels, Rag Irons, Ten Feet Wheel, Twelve do.do., Fourteen do.do., Eighteen do.do., Spurr Wheels, Dog Irons, etc." The only gudgeon I knew was a fish, but fish and iron, except when joined mouth to hook, were not usually found together. Immediately becoming curious about mill gudgeons, twere irons, mandrales, and the swedge black, I slapped the drawer back into the desk and set out for the library and nineteenth-century dictionaries.

Memories travel with people from house to house and, like possessions, fix thought and personality. Just when days bloom promising and one thinks he has slipped the weighty burden of the past, unwanted memory escapes from a trunk far back in the attic of the mind and glides across vision, shadowing perception and shackling mood. Along the boundary between my yard and that of a neighbor runs a long, deep row of forsythia. Every spring it is as yellow as butter, and when I look at it, my spirits soar, and for a moment life seems full of possibilities. But then my thought unconsciously travels back fifteen years to the Mountains of Gilead and groves of yellow acacia which bloom along the Amman-to-Damascus road. At first memory, like spring itself, is green. When the acacia blooms, families hire taxis and picnic along the Zarka River. The holiday becomes a day of courtship, gossip, and play. Old men and women sit in the shade on folding chairs. Young men whisper to their cousins, and children race about, breaking off branches of acacia and working them into the cars. Hoods become planters; grills and bumpers, trellises. All is festive, and by evening ordinary cars have become bright chariots of spring. Like the people themselves, though, memory cannot stay in one place. As the merrimakers must return to Amman and the owners of the taxis strip the acacia from their cars, so memory inexorably pushes north to Jerash. Once one of the league of free cities known as the Decapolis, Jerash is a ruin. Part of Roman grandeur, broken columns lie everywhere; still visible along the main street are ruts worn into paving stones by the wheels of countless chariots. Yet memory does not pull me to marble and dream; looking at the elegant, sweeping branches of forsythia, I see only the twisted hands of a beggar, and the promise of spring vanishes as I feel his thin fingers searching my face and hear him moan, "Backsheish, backsheish."

Much like memories, pictures and family frame life. A journey home is almost inevitably a return to the past. Former friends who haven't the energy or the inclination to consider one anew dredge up recollections. At home propriety must be meticulously observed. Old ladies have to be visited, and thank-you notes written for assorted canisters of chocolate-chip cookies. Conversations slip into a familiar pattern and, like chintz, become part of an acceptable formality. Days flow by so smoothly that one finds it difficult to believe he ever left home. Occasionally, when alone, one feels out of place, but the moment does not last. Little things swiftly turn thought into a channel of deep associations. A wrinkled black tie evokes balls and dinner dances and winter parties with girls as fresh as new Christmas trees. Climbing out of the past is almost impossible; association after association sweeps a person along, and leaving home is the only escape. Even after leaving, though, moving on is difficult. Strangers, as well as family and home, frame a person. Last spring I lectured in Birmingham. After my talk four professors from the University of Alabama and I went to dinner at a barbeque restaurant. Although the place was not fancy, it wasn't crude, and families occupied most of the tables. Wearing a gray suit, a blue necktie with white dots, and a cotton shirt with a button-down collar, I was formal, or at least was dressed in clothes which I thought would elevate me above the rough-hewn southern world I once knew. I was mistaken. When our waitress came over to the table, she stared at me and then, holding her pad and pencil in her left hand, stuck out her right hip and, boldly cocking her hand on her side, said, "What you boys are looking for isn't on the menu." I felt found out and despondent. Years of education and weary pursuit of things cultural had not changed me, at least from the waitress's point of view. Formal dress meant nothing to her. What she saw was just another southern male who, no matter how he labored to hide it behind sober grays and blues, had a red and raucous imagination.

Actually, framing by memories, possessions, and even strangers like the waitress may be more comforting than frustrating. Life rolls forever on, subjecting the individual to a string of jolts. Like the old ark in the spiritual, people are always "a-movering," often against their will. Facing cold mortality is hard; far warmer is the fiction that nothing, including the self, ever really changes. Recently my barber became ill. Taking time out only during the depression to work in a mill, Albert has cut hair for fifty-eight years. Albert is an old-fashioned barber, and going to him creates a comfortable sense of continuity. A haircut costs six dollars, and Albert spends an hour on each customer. No matter what instructions a person gives, however, he always gets the same haircut: the Christmas 1959 haircut, short all around, after which, my wife, Vicki, says, a person's "ears seem to stick up and then curl over at the top like leaves of rhubarb." No matter—the world of the Campus Barber Shop is familiar. Standing on a shelf before the mirror in front of Albert's chair are bottles of Osage Rub and Stephan's Dandruff Remover, three bottles of something called Nu-Vita, and a bottle of Noonan's Morning After Rub. Yesterday's issues of local newspapers, the *Willimantic Chronicle* and *Hartford Courant*, are piled loosely on a table. Some things, of course, are not quite as they were thirty years ago. The changes, however, are in particulars, not in tone. There are no crime magazines or bottles of Vitalis in the shop, and in all the years I have gone to

Albert, I have heard only one man ask for a flattop. Occasionally even a woman will appear and cut hair in the chair next to Albert. Wearing cowboy boots and a vest with sequins, she attracts undergraduates, talks loudly about parties, and charges twelve dollars. Happily, her disturbing presence never lasts longer than a season. By the next semester, she has moved somewhere trendy— to Shear Delight, Comb and Scissors, or The Kindest Cut of All— and the Campus Barber Shop settles back into the quiet rhythm of six-dollar haircuts. Since I get only three haircuts a year, Albert's health would appear to have little effect upon me. That is not true, however. Albert is the last of the old barbers in this part of Connecticut. If he died, I would have to go to a fashionable shop, a shop in which I would be uncomfortable and feel unframed, a place not of my days but of a world which has spun on and left me behind, marking hours and anticipating the end. No, no—far better to be sheared by Albert and see 1959 smiling at me from the mirror.

I have reached the age in which life totters. Instead of wanting days to pass quickly so that dreams can be realized, more often than not I want things to remain as they are. Early in December I discussed my essays on Connecticut Public Radio. The interview was good-natured, and near the conclusion the woman with whom I talked said, "You seem remarkably happy."

"Yes," I answered, "but happiness is fragile. Like a house of twigs, it can collapse in a moment. If anything were to happen," I continued, "to my baby girl, I don't think I could go on, much less be happy." The words made me nervous. I regretted saying them and wanted to take them back. Life moves on, and health doesn't last, but I did not want to think about that. Even before Eliza was born, my fears began; by giving me an actual child, fat and blue-eyed, birth only increased my worries.

Two days after the radio program, Eliza was feverish. A week passed and the fever came and went. We delayed taking her to the doctor, thinking her temperature would vanish in the doctor's office and we would return home, feeling foolish and carrying a prescription for Tylenol. One morning, though, Eliza had trouble hearing me; that afternoon we took her to the doctor, and she obliged us by running a temperature of 104.5. The doctor examined her carefully, but apart from the temperature, could find nothing wrong with her. As a precaution he took a sample of blood and then sending us home, saying she probably had a virus, instructed us to give her Tylenol. The next day Eliza's fever was gone, and we took her to a Christmas party at her brother's nursery school. The following afternoon she was in the hospital. She had a bug that caused childhood meningitis and a ward of terrible infections. The twigs had toppled, and as I sat beside Eliza in the dark, early morning hours watching medicine run slowly through a long tube into her arm, I remembered a drinking song from college:

> Our baby died last night;
> It died just for to spite us;
> It died of spinal meningitis.
> It was a lousy baby anyhow.

"My God," I thought, "how stupid and callous I was." But of course I wasn't stupid or callous; I was young and naive. I had no children and had never gone into a child's bedroom late at night as I do now every day. I had never really seen children sleeping— Francis spread out on his back with Elly, a stuffed elephant, under his left arm; Edward on his side, his right leg pulled up and his left arm around Teddy, his best friend; and little Eliza humped into a ball on green and yellow Winnie-the-Pooh sheets, her knees drawn under her, arms straight along her sides, and bottom in the air. I had never stood alone in the dark and felt terrible love and fear. On Eliza's second day in the hospital, I took a bag of toys to her room. I piled them around her to make her crib resemble home and create the illusions that she had never moved on and that she was not sick, or if she was, that everything would soon be as it had been.

By New Year's my little girl was healthy again, crawling from room to room and making thumping sounds like an aging washing machine. Life wasn't the same for me, however. "I'm walking on borrowed land," says the old spiritual. I had moved on, becoming more aware of the evanescence of everything. If such awareness stays in everyday thoughts, though, life becomes almost unbearable; and, drawing upon memory, I struggled to construct the fiction that things moved slowly. During my visit to Tennessee I asked Father to tell me more about characters he had known during his childhood in Carthage, people like Mr. Crittle. The town physician, Father began, was Dr. Jarrett. Until about noon Doctor Jarrett was fine, but then he started drinking. By two o'clock he had gone through a pint of whiskey and any diagnosis he made after two was likely to be unreliable. One afternoon about four, a farmer made the mistake of bringing his wife in for an examination. Dr. Jarrett gave her a quick once-over and then announced, "I hate to tell you, but you are heading for the last roundup." As could be expected, the doctor's manner exercised the couple considerably. Although the woman did not die for another twenty years, Doctor Jarrett was ultimately correct. Everybody is heading for the last roundup. Still, if one surrounds himself with family possessions, listens to old stories, and frequents the right sort of barber shop, he can occasionally create the comforting illusion that he and his children are not moving on to dust quite so fast as the folks down the road.

Son and Father

"The more I see of old people," my father said in the last letter he wrote me, "the greater my feeling is that the bulk of them should be destroyed."

"Not you," I thought when I read the letter, "at least not yet."

For years I imagined that I was different from, even better than, my father. Then one evening I walked into his room to ask about a book and found him asleep on his bed. Although I had seen him sleeping countless times, I was startled. His pajamas were inside out, as mine invariably are, and I noticed that we slept in the same position, left arm bent under the pillow, hand resting on the headboard; right leg pulled high toward the chest, and left thrust back and behind with the toes pointed, seemingly pushing us up and through the bed. Suddenly I realized Father and I were remarkably alike, the greatest difference being only the years that lay between us. At first I was upset. I had never consciously rejected family, but like the bottom of the bed against which I appeared to be pushing at night, my father and his life provided a firmness against which I could press and thrust myself off into something better.

As I looked at the old man lying on the bed, his thin ankles and knobby feet sticking out of his pajamas like fallen branches, I felt warm and comfortable. Instead of being parted by time and youth's false sense of superiority, we were bound together by patterns of living. His life could teach me about my future and my past, but, I thought, how little I knew about him. How well, I wondered, did any son know a father—particularly an only son, the recipient of so much love and attention that he worried about having a self and turned inward, often ignoring the parents about him and responding aggressively to concern with a petulant "leave me alone."

In his letter Father said that he and Mother disagreed about the past. "I tell her," he wrote, "that her recollections are remarkable, albeit not necessarily accurate." My memories of Father are ordinary and consist of a few glimpses: such things, for example, as his running alongside and steadying me when I learned to ride a bicycle and his fondness for chocolate. Mother liked chocolate too, and whenever Father was given a box of candy, he hid it in his closet where Mother could not reach it. The closet was dark, and as he grew older and his sight failed, he kept a flashlight in a shoebox. In a way, I suppose, past events resemble leaves on a tree. A multitude of little things make up life in full bloom, but as time passes, they fall and disappear without a trace. A few seeds blow into the garage, or memory, and get wedged behind spades, axes, and bits of lumber. If found or remembered, they are usually swept aside. Does it matter that Father rolled and chewed his tongue while telling a story or that after having drinks before dinner he would talk with his mouth full and embarrass me? Particular place is often necessary if the seeds lodged in memory are to sprout and grow green. Sadly, places vanish almost as quickly as leaves in October.

The Sulgrave Apartments, where I lived for eight years, and the long alley behind stretching through neighborhoods and drawing gangs of children to its treasures have vanished. When I was five I entered Ransome School. For the first months, Father walked all the way to school with me: along West End; across Fairfax, where Mr. Underwood the policeman waved at us; under the railway trestle and up Iroquois; past three small streets, Howell, Harding, and Sutherland. Slowly, as I grew surer, Father walked less of the distance with me; one morning he did not cross Sutherland; sometime later, he stopped at Harding, then Howell. Eventually he left me at the corner of Fairfax and I made my own way to Ransome under the watchful eye of Mr. Underwood. What I did when I was five, I can do no longer. The trestle and tracks with their caches of spikes, Iroquois, Harding, Howell, Sutherland, and Ransome itself, a scrapbook of small faces, have disappeared. All the associations that would freshen memory have been torn down for an interstate, going to Memphis or Birmingham, I am not sure which. Great washes of cars and trucks pour down ramps and rush through my old neighborhood. Traffic is so heavy that I rarely drive on West End, and when I must, the congestion makes me so nervous and the driving takes such concentration that I never think of Ransome, Mr. Underwood, or a little boy and a tall, thin man holding hands as they walked to school.

Father grew up in Carthage, Tennessee, a town of some two thousand people set high above the Cumberland River on red clay bluffs fifty-five miles east of Nashville. Since Carthage was the seat of Smith County, sidewalks ran along Main Street, and Father and his brother Coleman used to roller skate from their house to Grandfather's insurance agency, downtown over the bank. Life in Carthage was slow and from my perspective appealingly unsophisticated. On the front page of the weekly newspaper alongside an ad for Tabler's Buckeye Pile Ointment were excerpts from the sermons of the Reverend Sam P. Jones, the local Methodist minister. "I wouldn't give whiskey to a man until he had been dead for three days," Jones said. "When an old red-nosed politician gets so he isn't fit for anything else," he declared, "the Democrat Party send him to the Legislature." When a resident went away, a notice duly appeared on the front page. "D. B.

Kittrell," the paper informed readers, "went to Nashville last week with about 40 fat hogs and has not yet returned."

Not much money was to be made in Carthage, and people lived comfortably. Every morning Grandpa Pickering walked downtown and had coffee with friends, after which he came home for breakfast. Only then did he go to his office. Grandfather's house was a white, clapboard, two-story Victorian with a bright tin roof. A porch ran around two sides; at one corner of the porch was a cupola; on top was a weathervane. Huge sugar maples stood in the front yard, and about the house were bushes of white hydrangeas; in spring they seemed like mountains of snow to me. In back of the house was the well, sheds, fields, a tobacco barn, and then a long slope down to the river. Bessie the maid cooked Grandfather's breakfast. She made wonderful shortcake, and whenever I was in Carthage, she gave me sweet coffee to drink. Bessie's first marriage had not been a success; James, her husband, was unfaithful, and one night when he returned from gallivanting, she shot him. Although James lost a leg, he did not die, and Grandfather got Bessie off with a suspended sentence. Later, after Grandfather's death, Bessie married a preacher and moved to Nashville. On Thanksgiving and Christmas she often came to our house and cooked. The last time she came she asked me if I was still catching bugs and snakes.

I don't remember any snakes in Carthage, and the only bugs I recall catching are tobacco worms. I took a bucket from the back porch and after walking down to the tobacco patch filled it with worms. Then I drew a big circle in the dust on the road and in the middle dumped the worms. The first worm to detach itself from the squirming green pile and to crawl out of the circle I returned to the bucket and carried back to the field. The others I crushed. Tobacco worms are big and fat, and if I lined up worm and sole just right and put my foot down quickly heel to toe, I could occasionally squirt a worm's innards two feet.

Grandfather died when I was young, and I have few memories of him. During the last months of his life, he was bedridden.

Beside his bed was always a stack of flower magazines. All seemed to have been filled with pictures of zinnias, bright red and orange and occasionally purple zinnias, the only flower Father ever grew. Grandma Pickering outlived her husband, and I have clearer memories of her. She was strong-willed and opinionated, once confessing to me that she voted for Roosevelt the first time. In some ways Carthage may have been too small for her; she was interested in literature, and after her death I found scrapbooks filled with newspaper clippings, poems, reviews, and articles. Most of the poems were conventionally inspirational or religious and were typically entitled "Symbols of Victory" and "Earth Is Not Man's Abiding Place." Occasionally, though, I found other kinds of poetry, poems for the dreamer, not the moralist, poems which did not teach but which sketched moods. Pasted on the bottom of a page containing an article on "Shakespeare's Ideals of Womanhood" and a review of *For Whom the Bell Tolls* were two lines:

> I've reached the land of Golden-rod,
> Afar I see it wave and nod.

Much as it is hard to think of Father skating along the sidewalks of Carthage, so it is difficult to think of Grandma Pickering as a dreamer. Instead of bright, beckoning goldenrod, I associate her with a rusting red Studebaker. Almost until the day she died, she drove, and whenever she left Carthage for Nashville, the sheriff radioed ahead to the highway patrol, warning, "Mrs. Pickering's on the road." Along the way, patrolmen watched out for her, and when she reached Lebanon, one telephoned Father and then he and Mother and I drove out to a Stuckey's near the city limits and waited. After what seemed forever, she eventually appeared, inevitably with cars backed up behind her by the score, something that embarrassed me terribly.

Father told me little about his childhood in Carthage. I know only that he had an Airedale named Jerry; that on Rattlesnake Mountain, the hill just outside town, he once saw a huge snake;

that he almost died after eating homemade strawberry ice cream at a birthday party; and that Lucy, the talented little girl next door, died from trichinosis. Report cards provided most of what I know about Father's childhood, and in Grandmother's scrapbooks I found several. Father entered first grade in 1915; Lena Douglas taught him reading, spelling, writing, arithmetic, and language; his average for the year in all subjects was ninety-nine and a half; for his first two years he was remarkably healthy and only missed three days of school. The Carthage schools proved too easy, and for a year in high school Father attended KMI, Kentucky Military Institute, a place about which he never spoke except to say, "Children should not be sent to military schools." After KMI Father returned to Carthage, skipped two grades, graduated from high school, and in 1925 entered Vanderbilt.

One of my undergraduate nicknames was "Machine," and once or twice when I walked into class intent on an A, people made whirring or clanking sounds. Father, it seems, rarely attended class; every semester at Vanderbilt his quality credits were reduced because of absences. In 1927 he skipped so many classes that the dean called him in for a conference. Story had it that if the dean got out of his chair and put his arm around a student's shoulders, the student was certain to be dismissed from school. Midway through the interview, the dean rose and approached Father. Swiftly Father got up and walked around the desk, and thus conversation proceeded in circular fashion, with the dean lecturing and pursuing and Father explaining and running. The result was probation, not expulsion. It was a wonder that Father had enough energy to elude the dean, because he never attended gym class, a required course. Before graduation one of Father's physician friends wrote a letter, urging the suspension of the requirement in Father's case, explaining, "Pickering has a lameness in his back." After reading the letter, the dean said, "No more lies, Pickering; out of my office." Father left silently and graduated.

Although Father majored in English during the great years of

Vanderbilt's English department—the years of the Fugitives and the Agrarians—his college experiences were personal, not intellectual. From Carthage he brought with him the small-town world of particulars and familial relationships. For him, as for me, reality was apparent and truth clear, and he had little interest in hidden structures or highly wrought reasoning, making Ds in psychology and philosophy. In later years he rarely talked about classroom matters unless there was a story attached. When John Crowe Ransom assigned two poems to be written, Father exhausted his inspiration and interest on the first and got his roommate, who had a certain lyrical ability, to write the other. The week following the assignment, Professor Ransom read Father's two poems to the class, remarking, "It is inconceivable to me that the same person could have written these poems."

"A matter of mood, Mr. Ransom," Father explained, and he was right. Whose mood seems beside the point, especially when the nonpoetic have to write verse. I inherited Father's poetic skills, and in sixth grade when I was assigned a poem, I turned to him and he turned out "The Zoo," a very effective piece for twelve-year-olds, featuring, among other animals, a polar bear with white hair, a chimp with a limp, an antelope on the end of a rope, and a turtle named Myrtle. Despite his lack of poetic talent, Father read a fair amount of poetry and was fond of quoting verse, particularly poems like Tennyson's "The Splendour Falls," the sounds of which rang cool and clear like bells. Father's favorite poet was Byron; and the dying gladiator was a companion of my childhood, while the Coliseum seemed to stand not in faraway Rome but just around the corner of another day. College, however, probably had little to do with Father's enjoyment of Byron; the source was closer to home, Father's grandfather William Blackstone Pickering. On a shelf in our library I found *The Works of Lord Byron in Verse and Prose*, published in Hartford in 1840 by Silas Andrus and Son. The book was inscribed "Wm. B. Pickering from his father." Over the inscription a child wrote, "Sammie F. Pickering." Under that in a firm, youthful handwriting was written "Samuel Pickering, Beta House, Vanderbilt University, 1926."

Often holding three jobs at once, Father worked his way through Vanderbilt and simply did not have much time for classes. Yet he was always a reading man, and at times I suspected that there was nothing he had not read. Years later at his office, he kept books in the top drawer of his desk. When business was slow, he pulled the drawer out slightly, and after placing a pad and pencil in front of himself for appearances, he read. Despite the college jobs, such a reader should have done better than the Bs, Cs, and Ds Father made in English. In part the small-town world of Carthage may have been responsible for his performance. Carthage was a world of particulars, not abstractions, a place in which Tabler's Buckeye Pile Ointment "Cures Nothing but Piles," a town in which Mrs. Polk, a neighbor, could burst into Grandfather's kitchen crying that her daughter Mary, who had gone to Nashville, was "ruined."

"Oh, Lord," Grandfather exclaimed, "was she taken advantage of?"

"Yes," Mrs. Polk answered, "she had her hair bobbed."

At Vanderbilt during the 1920s literary criticism was shifting from the personal and anecdotal to the intellectual and the abstract. Instead of explaining ordinary life, it began to create an extraordinary world of thought far from piles and bobbed hair. For Father such a shift led to boredom and the conviction that although literary criticism might entertain some people, it was ultimately insignificant. In the sixty years that have passed since Father entered Vanderbilt, criticism has become more rarefied, and the result is, as a friend and critic wrote me, "we write books that even our mothers won't read."

Carthage influenced more than Father's school work; it determined the course of his career. Although Grandmother dreamed of the land of goldenrod, she stayed in Carthage and joined the Eastern Star. After graduating from Vanderbilt in 1929, Father went to work in the personnel department of the Travelers Insurance Company. Years later, he told me that he had made a mistake. "I did what my father did," he said; "I should have done something different, even run off to sea." An old man's thoughts often wander far from the path trod by the young man, and running away to sea is only accomplished in books and dreamed about when the house is quiet and the children asleep. For his insurance business, Grandfather traveled about Smith County in a buggy; occasionally he took the train to Nashville. Once when he was trying to settle a claim over a mule which had been struck by lightning (no mule ever died a natural death in Tennessee; mules were the lightning rods of the animal world), he stayed overnight at Chestnut Mound with Miss Fanny and Godkin Hayes. The next morning after breakfast, when he was climbing into his buggy, Miss Fanny asked Grandfather if he ever went to Difficult Creek, Tennessee, saying she had heard he was quite a traveler and had been to Nashville.

"Yes, ma'am," Grandfather answered. "I go there right much."

"Well, the next time you go," Miss Fanny said, "will you please say hello to Henry McCracken; he's my brother and I haven't seen him in over twenty years."

"What!" my grandfather exclaimed; "Difficult Creek is only twelve miles away, just on the other side of the Caney Fork River. Roane's Ferry will take you across in eight minutes."

"Oh, Mr. Sam," Miss Fanny answered wistfully, "I do want to see my brother, but I just can't bring myself to cross the great Caney Fork River."

Father crossed the Caney Fork, but he didn't travel far. After working in Washington and Richmond, he was sent to Nashville in the late thirties. From that time on he refused to be transferred. Beyond Difficult Creek lay the little town of Defeated Creek, and for most of his life Father was content to meander through a small circle of miles and visit with the Miss Fannys he met. Personnel, however, may have been too easy for him. Reading books in the office, he became a character, albeit a competent one. "He was a bumblebee," a man told me; "he shouldn't have been able to fly, but he did. What's more he did things that couldn't be done." By the 1960s, though, the topography of Father's world changed. The wild growth of wealth changed the course of Defeated Creek, making it swing closer to home. People suddenly became not who they knew or what they were but how much money they made. Strangers appeared, and instead of being identified by a rich string of anecdotes, they became bank accounts or corporations. It was almost impossible not to be swept up by the wash of money, and as Father's friends grew wealthy and began to possess the glittering goods of the world and to take trips beyond simple goldenrod to lands where orchids hung heavy from trees and butterflies bigger than fans waved in the sun, Father became envious. Although he occasionally criticized the affluence of certain groups—physicians, for example—he was not resentful. What troubled him most, I think, was how wealth changed conversation. Despite his wide reading, there was little room for him or Miss Fanny in talk about Bali or Borneo.

Disregard for possessions tempered Father's resentment of wealth. Although he liked shoes, both good and bad, and as a handsome man was vain on occasions like Christmas, when he wore a red vest, clothes, for example, mattered little to him. Outside the office he wore khaki trousers and checkered shirts that he bought at Sears. So long as the interior of the house was tasteful, something he knew Mother managed well, Father paid no attention to it. If a vistor admired something, Father was likely to offer it to him, especially, it seemed, if it was a family piece: an envelope of Confederate money or a Bible published in 1726 and listing forgotten generations of ancestors. As a child, I learned to hide things. When I found a box of old letters in a storeroom at Aunt Lula's house, I hid them in the attic. When the day came, as I knew it would, when Father asked for them, saying he had a friend who would like to have them, I lied and said that I lost them. Of course saving everything was beyond me, and I once resented his forays through my things. Even today when I want a good tricycle for my children, I resent his giving away the English trike that Mother's father bought me in New York. Now, though, I understand Father's desire to rid himself of possessions. I behave similarly. I wear Sears trousers and shirts from J. C. Penney's. I have turned down positions that would greatly increase my salary because I like the little out-of-the-way place where I live. I, too, alas, give away possessions. "You are the only teacher I have ever met," a graduate student told me recently, "who has two offices and not a single book." I don't have any books because I have given them away, out of, I think, the same compulsion that led Father to give away things and that kept him from becoming wealthy: the desire to keep life as clean and as simple as possible.

Wealth clutters life, bringing not simply possessions but temptation. Money lures one from the straight and clear into the darkly complex. The sidewalks in Carthage ran in narrow lines to the courthouse. Skating along them, a boy was always aware of where he was: in front of the Reeds' house, then the Ligons', the Fishers', the McGinnises', and then by the drugstore, the five and ten, King's barbershop, and finally the bank and post office. Wealth bends lines and makes it difficult for even the most adept skater to roll through life without losing his way or falling into the dirt. Instead of enriching, wealth often lessens life. At least that's the way I think Father thought, for he spurned every chance to become wealthy. For some twenty years he managed the affairs of his Aunt Lula, Grandmother's widowed sister. Father being her nearest relative, Aunt Lula called upon him whenever anything went wrong. For three summers in a row, Aunt Lula fell ill during Father's two-week summer vacation, and we hurried back to Nashville from the beach to put her in the hospital. Aunt Lula owned a farm, 750 acres of land just outside Nashville in Williamson County. The farm had been in the family for generations, and when I came home from college at Christmas, I spent mornings roaming over it rabbit hunting.

Aunt Lula did not have a will, and when Father's closest friend, a lawyer, learned this, he urged Father to let him draw one up for her. "For God's sakes, Sam," he said; "you have nursed her for years. She would want you to have the farm. I will make out the will tonight and you have her sign it tomorrow." Father demurred, and when Aunt Lula died, two relatives who had never met her shared the estate. Father put the land up for sale and received a bid of seventy-five thousand dollars.

"Borrow the money," Mother advised, "and buy the land yourself. Nashville is growing by leaps and bounds, and the farm is worth much more."

"That would not be right," Father answered, and the land was sold. Six years later it was resold for over a million dollars. Father kept the lines of his life straight and his temptations few, and I admire him for it; yet at night when I think about the three teaching jobs I have taken this summer so the house can be painted and dead oaks felled in the yard, I sometimes wish he had not sold the farm. This is not to say that Father did not understand the power of money. He thought it important for other people and urged me to make the most of my chances, citing his younger brother Coleman as a warning. According to Father, Coleman was the talented Pickering and could have done practically anything; yet, Father recounted, he refused to grasp opportunities. Satisfied to live simply, Coleman was in truth Father's brother, a man wary of complexity, determined to remain independent and free from entangling responsibilities.

After forty most people I know realize that their actions and thoughts are inconsistent. Worried about gypsy moths, a child's stuttering, or slow-running drains, they have little time for principle and not simply neglect but recognize and are comfortable with the discrepancy between words and deeds. To some extent Father's attitude toward wealth reflected this state of mind. Behind his behavior, however, also lay the perennial conflict between the particular and the abstract or the general. From infancy through school people are taught the value of general truths or principles, the sanctity, for example, of honor and truth itself. As one grows older and attempts to apply principles to real human beings, one learns that rules are cruelly narrow and, instead of bettering life, often lead to unhappiness. The sense of principle or belief in general truth is so deeply ingrained, however, that one rarely repudiates it. Instead, one continues to pay lip service to it and actually believe in its value while never applying it to particular individuals. Thus during the turmoil over integration in Nashville during the 1950s and early '60s, Father sounded harshly conservative. One day, though, while he and Mother and I were walking along Church Street, we came upon four toughs, or hoods as they were then called, harassing a black woman. "You there," Father bellowed, all 136 pounds of him swelling with his voice; "who do you think you are?" Then as mother and I wilted into a doorway, he grabbed the biggest tough and, shaking him, said, "Apologize to this lady. This is Tennessee, and people behave here."

"Yes, sir, yes, sir," the man responded meekly and apologized.

Father then turned to the woman, and while the toughs scurried away, took off his hat and said, "Ma'am, I am sorry for what happened. You are probably walking to the bus stop; if you don't mind, my wife and I and our son would like to walk with you."

Although Father expounded political and moral generalities during the isolation of dinner, he never applied them to the hurly-burly of his friends' lives. He delighted in people too much to categorize and thus limit his enjoyment of them. Not long after the incident on Church Street, Father was invited to join the Klan. Around ten or eleven each morning, a man appeared outside the Travelers building, selling doughnuts and sweet rolls. As could be expected from a man who did not have to work too hard and who loved candy, Father always bought a doughnut and a cup of coffee and then chatted a bit. On this occasion, the man said, "Mr. Pickering, I have known you for some time, and you seem a right thinking man. This Friday there is going to be a meeting of the Klan at Nolensville, and I'd like for you to attend and become a member."

"That's mighty nice of you to invite me," Father replied, "but I believe I will just continue to vote Republican."

As could be expected, Father was inconsistent toward me. Of things he thought comparatively unimportant—sports, for example—he rarely said much, except to moan about the Vanderbilt football team. When I was in high school, he picked me up after football practice, and unlike some boys' fathers, who filmed practices, had conferences with the coaches, and caused their sons untold misery, Father never got in the way. About social matters he behaved differently, urging me to do the things he never did—join service clubs, for example. "They will help your career," he explained. When he heard me taking a political stance that was not generally accepted and thereby safe, he intervened. Ten years ago I spent three months in the Soviet Union. On my return people often asked me questions; once during a discussion with businessmen Father overheard me say something "risky." "Pay no attention to my son," he interrupted; "he has been brainwashed." That ended the conversation.

Of Father's courtship of Mother, I know and want to know little. Toward the end of his life, he refused to tell me family stories, saying, "You will publish them." Quite right—I would publish almost anything except an account of his and Mother's love affair. Theirs was a good and typical marriage with much happiness and sadness during the early and middle years and with many operations at the end. They were very different, but they stumbled along in comparative harmony.

"When I first met him," Mother told me; "I thought him the damnedest little pissant."

"Your mother," Father often said, "does not appreciate my sense of humor." That was a loss, because laughing was important to Father, and for much of his life, he played practical jokes.

Practical jokes are an almost implicit recognition of the foolishness of man's endeavors. Involving actual individuals rather than comparative abstractions like word play, for example, such humor flourishes in stable communities in which people's positions remain relatively constant and clearly defined. The popularity of practical jokes waned as the South grew wealthy. Money undermined community both by making people more mobile and by changing the terms by which position was defined. As people became financial accomplishments, not neighbors, cousins, sons, and daughters, they took themselves more seriously. When they, rather than a web of relationships over which they had comparatively little control, determined what they were, their actions grew increasingly significant. No more could the practical joker be seen as a friend; no more was his laughter benign, even fond. Instead, threatening the basis of identity by mocking, he undermined society. By the late 1960s Father had stopped playing practical jokes; before then, though, the going was good.

After selling some rocky, farmed-out land to a company that wanted to construct a shopping center, one of Father's acquaintances, Tuck Gobbett, built a twenty-room house outside Nashville. Known locally as the Taj Mahal, the house had everything: sauna bath, swimming pool, Japanese shoji screens around the garage, and even a pond with swans purchased from a New York dealer. In its garishness the house was marvelous, and Father enjoyed it, saying only, "The birds were a mistake. As soon as snapping turtles find the pond, it's good-bye swans." He was right; two years later the turtles came, and the swans disappeared. Father decided Gobbett went too far, however, when he got rid of the off-brand beagles he had always owned and bought an Afghan hound. The dog had a royal pedigree, and when Gobbett advertised in a kennel-club magazine that the dog was standing at stud, Father saw his chance. "Why is it," he asked me years later, "that mongrel people always want pure-bred dogs." Father then read about Afghans, learning quite a bit about blood lines. Able to disguise his voice, he telephoned Gobbett, explaining that he lived in Birmingham and was the owner of a champion bitch. He had, he said, seen the advertisement in the kennel-club magazine and wondered about the possibility of breeding the animals. Of course, he continued, he would first have to scrutinize the pedigree of Gobbett's dog. After Gobbett detailed his dog's ancestry, Father then supplied that of the bitch, which, not surprisingly, came from the best Afghan stock in the nation. Saying he would need time to investigate the Gobbetts' dog, Father hung up, promising to call within a week. During the week Father visited Gobbett. When asked about news, Gobbett excitedly described the telephone call, saying the bitch had "an absolutely first-class pedigree" and the puppies would be worth a thousand dollars apiece.

The next week Father telephoned, saying he looked into the dog and thought the pedigree would do. Although the owner of the bitch usually received all the puppies except for one from a breeding, Father said he did not want a single puppy. After this remark, he said he had pressing business and would call the following week to make arrangements for the mating. Gobbett was ebullient. "What fools there are in the world," he said; "there is money to be made in these dogs. The puppies will make me a man to be reckoned with in Afghan circles." As could be expected, completing the arrangements was not easy, but after a month and a half of conversations, the date and place were set. Then at the end of the final telephone call, almost as an afterthought, Father said, "There is just one thing though."

"What's that?" Gobbett asked.

"Oh, nothing important," Father said; "my dog has been spayed, but I don't suppose that will make a difference."

Father's humor was rarely bawdy, and the jokes he told were usually stories, gentle tales about foolishness. My favorite, one that I have often told, was called "Edgar the Cat." Two bachelor brothers, Herbert and James, lived with their mother and James's cat Edgar in a little town not unlike Carthage. James was particularly attached to Edgar, and when he had to spend several days in Nashville having work done on his teeth, he left Herbert meticulous instructions about Edgar. At the end of his first day away from home, James telephoned Herbert. "Herbert," he said, "how is Edgar?"

"Edgar is dead," Herbert answered immediately.

There was a pause; then James said, "Herbert, you are terribly insensitive. You know how close I was to Edgar and you should have broken the news to me slowly."

"How?" Herbert said.

"Well," James said, "when I asked about Edgar tonight, you should have said 'Edgar's on the roof, but I have called the fire department to get him down.'"

"Is that so?" said Herbert.

"Yes," James answered, "and tomorrow when I called you could have said the firemen were having trouble getting Edgar down but you were hopeful they would succeed. Then when I called the third time you could have told me that the firemen had done their best but unfortunately Edgar had fallen off the roof and was at the veterinarian's, where he was receiving fine treatment. Then when I called the last time you could have said that although everything humanly possible had been done for Edgar he had died. That's the way a sensitive man would have told me about Edgar. And, oh, before I forget," James added, "how is mother?"

"Uh," Herbert said, pausing for a moment, "she's on the roof."

There was an innocence in Father's humor, perhaps a sign of softness, something that contributed to his not grabbing Aunt Lula's farm. In the eighteenth and early nineteenth centuries, Pickerings were Quakers and, so far as I call tell, gentle people who did not struggle or rage against life but who took things as they came, people who copied poems into family Bibles while recording the deaths of children. When seven-year-old Marthelia died in 1823, her father wrote:

When the Icy hand of death
  his sabre drew!
To cut down the budding
  rose of morn!!
He held his favorite motto
  full in view—
The fairest Bud must the
  tomb adorn!!!

In general Pickerings lived quiet lives, cultivating their few acres and avoiding the larger world with its abstractions of honor, service, and patriotism. For them country meant the counties in which they lived, not the imperial nation. Years ago I knew John Kennedy had things backwards when he said, "Ask not what your country can do for you, but what you can do for your country." The great excuse for country, with its borders dividing brothers, was that it bettered the life of the individual.

With the exception of the Civil War, the struggles of the nation have not touched us. Coming of age between battles, few Pickerings have looked at the dark side of man's heart. Perhaps because of this, we are soft and, in our desires, subconscious or conscious, to remain free, have become evasive. Few things are simple, though, and this very evasiveness may be a sign of a shrewd or even tough vitality. Aware that those who respond to challenges and fight for a cause or success often are ground under, we have learned to live unobtrusively and blossom low to the ground and out of sight. Even when a Pickering does respond to a call, it's usually not for him. In 1942 the navy rejected Father's application for Officers' Training School because he was too thin. In 1944 Father was drafted; two days before he was slated to leave for training camp and after a series of farewell parties, he received a telegram instructing him not to report, explaining that he was too thin.

Not long ago my daughter Eliza McClarin Pickering was born.

She was born, fittingly enough, in a hospital in a relatively small town. For four days she was the only baby in the maternity ward, and the nurses let me wander in and out at my convenience. With little to do, the nurses drank coffee, ate doughnuts, and talked. One night as I stood looking at Eliza in her crib, I overheard a conversation at the nurses' station around the corner. "I have worked at four hospitals," one nurse declared confidentially, "but this is the worst for poking I have ever seen. There's Shirley," she said, warming to the subject, "she runs out to the parking lot and gets poked every chance she gets. And Kate, there's not a bed on the third floor that she hasn't been poked in." Like Homer's account of those slain at the sack of Troy, the nurse's list of fallen was long and colorful. During the recital, the second nurse was silent. Finally, though, she spoke. "My word," she said in mild astonishment, "it's just a whirlwind of festivities."

Although few strong breezes blow through the lives of Pickerings, there are festivities, not shining affairs strung with bright lights but quiet events lit by words. After being married on my grandfather's farm in Hanover, Virginia, Father and Mother spent their first night together in the Jefferson Hotel in Richmond. Early the next morning they started for Nashville in Father's Ford coupe. On the outskirts of Richmond, they stopped for gas, and Mother bought a newspaper to look at the wedding pictures. She spread the paper out on the front seat and was looking at the pictures with Father when the man who was cleaning the windshield spoke up, saying, "It's a pity about that wedding. I feel so sorry for the girl."

"What do you mean," Father answered, jumping in before Mother could respond.

"Well," the man said, "she didn't marry the man she wanted to. She was in love with a poor insurance man but her father made her marry a rich fellow."

"Who told you that?" Father asked.

"Oh," the man answered, "a colored preacher that comes

through here told me all about it. He preaches up in Hanover, and some of the members of his congregation work at her father's farm."

"Hmmm," Father said, "I hate to ruin your story, but look at the picture of the groom, and then look at me. This," he said gesturing toward Mother after the man had a good look, "is that unfortunate girl, and I am the poor insurance man. The preacher was wrong; sometimes in life poor folks carry off the prizes." And that's what Father did in a quiet way all his days. No prize of his was mentioned in an obituary; his name was not associated with any accomplishment; yet in the few acres he tilled and even beyond, at least as far as Carthage, he was known.

While at Vanderbilt, Father bought an old car. On a trip to Carthage it broke down, and, having to hurry back to Nashville to take an examination, one of the few times he attended class, Father left the car in Carthage and took the train. For a modest fee George Jackson, a black man, agreed to drive the car to Nashville once it was repaired. Father wrote out careful instructions and drew a map. Alas, George lost both, but this did not deter him. On arriving in Nashville, he stopped in a residential area, went up to a house, and asked where "young Mr. Samuel Pickering" lived. Amazingly, the people in the house knew Father. They gave George clear directions, and he delivered the car. When Father learned that the map had gone astray and George had lost his way, he asked him how he knew whom to ask for instructions. "Mister Sam," George answered, "everybody knows you." The one time Father told this story, he laughed, then said, "What a world we have lost. Not a better world," he added, "but a different one. At times I miss it." Not, old man, so much as I miss you—not so much as I miss you.

My Writing Life

This fall a collection of my essays appeared. "Put the book on a table in the living room," my friend Jay said, "and when someone sees it, he will say, 'I didn't know you were a writer,' and then you can answer, 'Oh, yes—yes, indeed.' Aside from your mother and father and friends to whom you gave books," Jay added, "that's about all the attention you will get." Jay was right and wrong. Although the book received little national attention, I have become known locally. When Vicki and I took our children around the neighborhood on Halloween, four of the people who asked us in for treats identified me as "our writer." Before then I was their layabout. On warm afternoons, I make a pot of tea and carry it and an old yellow-and-white lawn chair out to the end of the driveway. While my children play in the yard, I sit, drink tea, wave at joggers, and chat with people walking to and from work. Of course, I did have silly prepublication moments. Sometimes late in the summer, while I dozed in the lawn chair, a screen clicked on in my mind and I dreamed of being more than just the writer at the end of the driveway. I imagined myself in a busy airport, stopping a stranger bustling to his next flight.

"Do you know me?" I asked.

For a moment the stranger seemed irritated, but then, like the sun poking through clouds after a storm, recognition broke across his face. "Do I know you!" he exclaimed. "Hell, yes! What a tomfool question! You are Sam Pickering."

"That's right," I said, flipping my charge card into a waste can and taking out my pen to sign an autograph.

Unless a person is a professional, bartering words for Wonder Bread, writing is one of the insignificant things done in life. Pen and paper have little to do with important matters. Being a decent husband and son, treating children kindly, raking leaves, mowing grass, and taking the garbage out on Tuesday mornings are the things that fill hours and bring contentment. Still, I do write, and writing had made some difference in my life. During a snowstorm last Friday, a photographer came to the house. The usual coat-and-tie, living-room or study picture was not for him. Wanting something revealingly poetic, he posed me outside next to the woodpile. To add color to the picture, I wore a thin red sweater instead of my down jacket. While the snow caught in my hair, melted, and then ran down my neck, pooling under my shirt, half-freezing my nipples off, I stood sideways, hand on hip, foot on log, and looked off into the distance as if searching for inspiration, rather than warmth. The picture has yet to appear, and I have no idea if it will increase the sales of my book. What it has brought, however, is midwinter catarrh, a snorting, coughing, deep-chested, rumbling catarrh.

A bookstore of sales could not make my cough worthwhile. In any case, my sales will never be large. Over the past five years writing has brought me $11,653, and this is before expenses are deducted and includes fees for talks and readings. Writing has influenced my reading as well as my health. As I labor to describe my actual world, so I now want to read about ordinary life. No longer do I have patience for the abstract and the otherworldly. I am convinced that if life has any meaning at all, such meaning occurs as one struggles here and now, feet planted firmly on the dark, sustaining earth. Once upon a time, romance charmed me, and I passed endless hours wandering along the golden banks of fairy land. Now fairy tales offend me. Of course I can't always control my thoughts, and occasionally the matter of romance attracts me. Trains, for example, still fascinate me, and not long ago a picture of a train crossing a high trestle with smoke billowing behind like a cloud caught my eye. The picture was part of an advertisement for a tour company. "Follow in the Tracks of Kings, Smugglers, Lovers and Spies," the company urged, take the Orient Express from Paris to Istanbul and travel "to the ends of the earth. And beyond." Along the way travelers could visit Dracula's birthplace, attend "an opulent ball in a Viennese palace," and enjoy "a gourmet dinner in a former sultan's hunting lodge." As I looked at the picture, I imagined the train steaming through the night, its whistle blowing long and blue. For a moment romance had me in her grasp and I left the real behind and wandered through the beyond. The beyond, though, is no place for a man with three small children. The enchantment did not last long; soon I was back with the good and the true, diapers and pins, and crayons and blocks. Trains are made to carry people not out of this world, but through it. Not for me the misty regions of Transylvania or the sultan's magic carpet. On real trains that roll through lands with strange-sounding names, days are ordinary. Traveling from Cairo to Luxor, one does not meet kings or spies but bed bugs; on cars from Belgrade to Athens one does not embrace love, brightly a-jangle, but painted disease.

Instead of carrying me beyond, writing, like reading, has thrust me against the actual. My essays are not found in smugglers' backpacks or on the well-lit shelves of a king's library. Ordinary people read my essays and write me about their lives. "Quite by chance," a woman recently wrote from Ohio, "I happened to see your book *Continuing Education* in the window of the bookstore in the town where I shop. I must confess," she explained, "I am not a book reader especially, though I did spend two years in a college here in Ohio. I have always had an interest nonetheless in continuing my own education, so I went into the store (impulse!) and bought your book." A collection of personal essays instead of a manual suggesting how people who had left school could continue to grow, the book initially disappointed the woman. Still she read on, explaining she found the essays "strangely interesting." In the next-to-last essay in the book was a small section in which the narrator, a fictional I, at that time a young college student, received a letter from a girl named Annie, saying she was pregnant. "You will be quite surprised, I am sure," my correspondent wrote, "to know the truth of something. My name is Ann (no *e*) and I, in my second year of college in Ohio (a Christian Bible College, the name of which shall remain anonymous) made the same mistake that your little Annie made. I had sex intercourse several times with a senior. His name, which startles me, was Sam, too. How could something like this happen. This, after all, was forty years ago. I did go ahead and give birth to a child, a little boy, who I called (after his daddy), Sam. It's all so odd. Little Sam died seven months later, maybe it was what they now call crib death. At the time, the doctor had no cause. Like the boy just didn't want me, either." The woman signed the letter, carefully putting "Miss" before her name, and included a return address.

Heavy with love lost and life missed, the letter bothered me. When I receive a letter, I usually answer it the next day. This time, though, I waited for a week before responding. Words, like the actions of the woman's lover years ago, seemed inadequate. Still, I tried to convey warmth and light. "The coincidences are remarkable and remarkably sad," I wrote; "your letter touched me, and memories flooded over me like tears." Then after recounting a couple of gentle, smiling stories, I ended with "God Bless You." The next morning I mailed the letter; nine days later, it was back, stamped "Returned to Sender. Attempted. Not Known." The letter's being returned puzzled me. Why did the woman give a false address? If she wanted to remain unknown, wouldn't it have been simpler to have left the letter unsigned and not have included any address? Although I thought about the incident for some time, I came to no conclusions, and that perhaps is the way things should be. Unlike the tourist experience, life cannot be neatly and opulently packaged.

Only rarely are responses to my writing so poignant. Usually my essays bring laughter and embarrassment, and in the case of embarrassment, usually to me. The more successful the writing, the more attention one receives and greater are the chances that one will do or say something foolish. Some months ago I was interviewed by a radio station in Hartford. When the interview was broadcast, Vicki and I tuned in. Hartford, however, is thirty-five miles from our house, and our radio doesn't work well. In order for us to hear the program, Vicki had to put one hand on the radio and rest her other hand against the cabinet on which the radio sat. For my part I was forced to stand in the middle of the kitchen and hold the icebox door open. If the door shut or Vicki took a hand away, the broadcast disintegrated into static. For fifteen minutes, all, including me, went well. But then I said, "There's a little sex in the book because there used to be a little sex in my life." At that point static began. "I can't believe you said that on the radio," Vicki said, taking her hand off the cabinet; "suppose some of our friends heard that. What will they think?"

Little things like tone and detail make writing good. Similarly, the more I write, the more convinced I am that little things make life good. In my essays past experiences are important, and before I write I spend time thinking through the past. Invariably what comes to mind are not big but little events. Perhaps the very bigness of some memories makes them too difficult to comprehend, while, in contrast, the significance of something small is relatively clear. Whatever the reason, though, the little things in my past, and now in my present, seem more important than ever before. What was once simply the stuff of humor has become tellingly and revealingly important. What I remember most fondly about graduate school are not classroom hours when ideas glittered like sparklers. Instead I recall the generosity of a janitor.

My childhood was privileged. My parents were not wealthy, but I was never in want. Whatever I needed, they provided, and more. More because aside from books and the fees associated with a long education, I never asked for much. Clothes in particular hold little attraction for me, and I have always been most comfortable in the wrinkled and the frayed. By making it easy to slip off and on, missing buttons did not lessen but only increased the frequency with which I wore a shirt. Once trousers were torn, they became beat-around clothes, and since all I ever did was beat around, I wore torn trousers every day. One morning, though, after I had been at Princeton for four months, the head janitor at the Graduate College appeared at my door. In his arms was a bundle of clothes. "Sam," he began, "I know what it is like to be poor and not have good clothes. I lost everything during the war, and when I came to this country from Latvia, people were wonderful. They gave me clothes and got me this job. I now own a house, and both my children have graduated from college. You remind me," he continued, "of myself when I first came here, and I want you to have these clothes." The man's kindness was wondrous, and after thanking him profusely, I took the clothes. The problem, however, was that I was over six feet and skinny, and he was five-eight and fat. When I put his trousers on, the behind hung down like a watermelon and the front pouched out like an oven stuffed with a turkey. The legs stopped two inches above my ankles, but all this was a small matter when compared to the way his sweater fit. It first gathered about my neck like a football player's shoulder pads, and then after hanging down for three inches or so, bunched up over my chest, giving me a formidable, albeit wrinkled and stringy, bosom. Of course, how the clothes fit was beside the point. What mattered was the man's generosity and his feelings. I had to wear the clothes, and wear them I did, at least twice a week until the janitor retired two and a half years later.

Along with leading me to think about the past, writing has made me more observant. I carry a pencil and a scrap of paper wherever I go; if I hear or see something that strikes my interest, I jot it down. Again little things seem to have become increasingly significant, and I am forever looking for right details. Two weeks ago I ate dinner in a small family restaurant along the railway tracks in Gainesville, Florida. Thinking that someday I might describe the meal in an essay, I wrote down what I ate for dinner. For the main course I had fried chicken livers and gizzards; with the dinner came three vegetables, and I had fried eggplant, okra mixed with corn and stewed tomatoes, and fried "Turnep Roots." For dessert I ate sweet potato bread. In the motel the next morning at breakfast, my waitress called grits "Georgia Ice Cream," and I wrote that down, too.

In the hope of picking up useful details, I always chat with waitresses. A password is not enough to get someone by me. I want more. The man assigned the seat next to me on an airplane won't reach his destination without having first told me about his life. When an opportunity for me to begin a conversation does not arise, I listen to the conversations of others. Much that I overhear is memorable, but not all is suitable for an essay. Last summer I attended a performance of *Coppelia* at Royal Festival Hall in London. Seated on my immediate left were two strikingly well-dressed English women. They appeared knowledgeable about ballet, and during the course of the first act, they frequently consulted their programs and whispered to each other. Although I enjoy ballet, I am not sensitive to the finer points of dance, and in hopes of picking up a subtlety or two, I tried to listen to their conversation at intermission. Unfortunately, they left their seats to get a glass of wine, and I only managed to hear a single remark before they left. As the curtain came down, one woman turned to the other and said, "My word, yes, he does have a very large cock."

Much as I note conversations, so whenever I read now, I have a pencil at hand, ready to copy down anything that might prove usable in an essay. Readers who write enjoy "toten privileges," and, like the sitting room of an old and honored servant, my essays are cluttered with things which once belonged to others. Unhappily, not everyone approves of toten, and whenever someone behaves like the devil in Amen Corner and refuses to say "So be it," I tell a story about an incident that I say occurred near the turn of the century in Carthage, Tennessee. Of course, the story did not take place in Carthage; I toted it out of a book of folk tales and set it in Carthage. Prunty Boon, I begin, was the town ne'er-do-well. Although his daddy, J. P. Boon, had been a prosperous blacksmith, Prunty was too lazy to be any account and got along by "borrowing." If a rightful owner ever objected to his borrowing something, Prunty returned it, and so for years he ambled comfortably along just the other side of the law. This changed, though, when Stainsby Simms moved up from Nashville to sell insurance and Prunty borrowed his wagon the day before Simms was supposed to drive into the country and discuss insurance with Washtell Utney, owner of the biggest farm in Smith County. Angry because he missed his appointment and Washtell bought insurance from someone else, Simms took Prunty to court. Never before had Prunty's borrowings led to the courthouse, and, not sure how to plead, Prunty showed up early and studied what other people did. The two cases before Prunty's were straightforward. Accused of stealing a horse, the first defendant pleaded not guilty, and the judge dismissed the case when the man said, "I have owned that horse since he was a colt." The second man was accused of stealing a cow, but his case was dismissed after he said, "I have owned that cow since she was a calf." Prunty now saw the way out, and when the judge asked him how he pleaded, he said, "Not guilty, your honor; I have owned that wagon since it was a wheelbarrow."

At the end of the story, I plead not guilty myself, saying that although what I toted might have been in print before, I have owned it since it was a rough mess of nouns, conjunctions, adverbs, adjectives, and all the rest. If a person still objects and mumbles about plagiarism, then I raise my voice and, borrowing something from the old Hoosier philosopher Abe Martin, say, "You have been reading too much of the Good Book. To succeed in this world, you have to be a little bad. Great God!" I exclaim, "if the meek ever do inherit the earth, someone will get it away from them before they have had it an hour." If this doesn't silence him, then I try to blast him off principle with a barrage from Josh Billings. "Mr. Man," I say, "was created only a little lower than the angels. But one day before he was weaned, he was frisking about and fell out of his cradle. Years have rolled by, and although Mr. Man has got himself a gray beard, he is still falling, and if the truth be known, he is a long way from striking bottom. If you let my little borrowings upset you, you are going to have a hard time getting over the big jolts ahead. Look," I say, suddenly acting concerned, "the only way to be happy in this world is to take things as they come and let them go just the same way."

Not only do people overrate writing, but they rate the satisfaction it brings too highly, thinking of writing as a hardy imperishable. In truth words fall from sight faster than early tulips, and the pleasure writing provides is fragile. Whenever I see an essay of mine in print, I am surprised. Not only can I not remember much about writing it, but the essay always seems to have been written by a stranger. Usually I don't read the essay and quickly move on to something else. As in all hobbies, the seeds of dissatisfaction lie deep within writing, waiting for the right combination of age and cloud to bring them to fruition. When I started writing years ago, I had a study on the third floor of the library at Dartmouth College. Four doors down from me, an emeritus professor, Haynie Givner, had a study. Every day when I came in after class, Haynie was at work. Late in the afternoon when I left for home and dinner, Haynie was still at work. Three years passed, and then one morning Haynie came into my study. His shoulders were hunched over, and tears ran down his face.

"Sam," he cried, "I don't know what to do. This morning I finished my book."

"Haynie," I said, "that's splendid."

"No," he answered, "you are too young and don't understand. For six years I have worked on the book. If the publisher rejects it, I will have worked six years for nothing. But if he accepts it, I won't have anything left to do, and my life will be over."

I didn't know how to act, so I put my arm over Haynie's shoulder and said, "Don't worry, Haynie, you will find something else to write about." I was wrong, and Haynie was right; I was too young to understand. Haynie had nothing else to say. After he mailed his manuscript off, I never saw him in the library again, and soon someone else had his study. I would like to avoid Haynie's fate, but that's probably impossible. The best I can do is not take writing seriously and have fun: reading, listening to stories, and taking notes. One of the local newspapers ran an article about me recently, and when Vicki picked Francis up at nursery school last week, a woman said to her, "I didn't know your husband was a writer. What's it like being married to a writer?"

"No different from being married to a carpenter or a plumber," Vicki answered, "except they work harder. If you are really curious, wait until warm weather and then you can talk to Sam yourself. Drive by the house some sunny afternoon. He is sure to be out at the end of the driveway, sitting in his lawn chair, drinking tea, waving at joggers, and chatting with neighbors."